Heidegger and Moral Realism

Heidegger and Moral Realism

ANOOP GUPTA

☙PICKWICK *Publications* • Eugene, Oregon

HEIDEGGER AND MORAL REALISM

Copyright © 2015 Anoop Gupta. All rights reserved. Except for brief quotations in critical publications or reviews, no part of this book may be reproduced in any manner without prior written permission from the publisher. Write: Permissions, Wipf and Stock Publishers, 199 W. 8th Ave., Suite 3, Eugene, OR 97401.

Pickwick Publications
An Imprint of Wipf and Stock Publishers
199 W. 8th Ave., Suite 3
Eugene, OR 97401

www.wipfandstock.com

ISBN 13: 978-1-4982-0378-4

Cataloguing-in-Publication Data

Gupta, Anoop.

    Heidegger and moral realism / Anoop Gupta.

    xiv +180 p. ; 23 cm. Includes bibliographical references and index.

    ISBN 13: 978-1-4982-0378-4

    1. Heidegger, Martin, 1889–1976—Criticism and interpretation. 2. Moral realism. I. Title.

B3279.H49 G86 2015

Manufactured in the U.S.A.   11/09/2015

For PJ. For sorrow I caused along the way, and the joy that is you.

In the end we search out beginnings.

—Solomon Feferman,
commenting on Kurt Gödel's life

Contents

Preface | ix
Acknowledgments | xi
Abbreviations | xii

Prologue: A Heideggerian Ethics and Yesterday | 1

Part I: Everyday Ethics
1. Ends and Origins | 9
2. Ethical Thinking | 18
3. Back to Before Kant | 25
4. Romanticism Revisited | 31

Part II: Interlude: Being and Ethics
5. Ethics and Time | 49
6. Ontological Similarity | 57

Part III: Contrasts and Reflections
7. Kant's Conundrum | 73
8. Hegel's Aesthetics | 82
9. Schweitzer's Ethics | 93
10. A Heideggerian Rebuttal of Ethical Relativism | 106
11. Heidegger and Ethical Naturalism | 115
12. Prospects for Moral Realism | 141

Bibliography | 149
Index | 161

Preface

The main purpose of religion is to get rid of doubt, not to increase it. As we can read in the Bhagavad Gita: "There is no pleasure for the doubting self—not in this world or the next."[1] Strategically, doubt has its uses to be sure, but as a global worldview, it is nothing most would choose.

A large part of what Heidegger offered is a critique of modernity. He can help us diagnosis, for instance, some of the reasons that led to the fall of metaphysics. He can help us understand, specifically, I shall argue, why moral realism largely fell out of favor, when modernity reached its apex, that is, before it collapsed. There is also a positive point. By pursing a Heideggerian ethics may open a way—by our success or failure to develop such an account—to moral realism. If Heidegger will not get us to moral realism, we may find some other way or get to know how far we can plausibly go in that direction. Those of a realist persuasion have a friend in my interpretation of Heidegger's writings and this project.

My concern with Heidegger and realism stems from a dissatisfaction with the conventionalism resulting from the decline of metaphysics, which has been inspired, for example, by Wittgenstein. Furthermore, like many realists, I think that the rampant anti-realism is a sign of the times. The prevalence of anti-realism is at least telling to the particular state of philosophy, a bad state, and perhaps even our intellectual life in general.

Some European philosophers, under heavy influence of the French, stand aghast at the notion that Heidegger could be interpreted to be a defender of ethical or metaphysical realism. Further, some English philosophers, no doubt, would see the flight to Heidegger as a mark of how bankrupt realism may be. I do not contend that there may be other ways

---

1. *Gita*, 4.40.

PREFACE

to moral realism than a study of Heidegger's writings or that there are not better routes to a more detailed realism in general.

After all, Heidegger often did not criticize specific arguments; rather, he attempted to show how framing questions in a certain way are part of a larger crisis that occurred in the history of the West. Yet failures can sometimes lead to other successes, just as successes can lead to other failures. So I request that we suspend judgement about a Heideggerian ethics at the outset only.

Heidegger arrived at the precipice. Heidegger captures the dual suspicion of modernity that animated, for instance, the Romantics. First, not only was he critical of scientism, philosophically, he also provides a critique of what underlies the rise of modern scepticism. Second, Heidegger, assumes, as did the Romantics, a moral vision of how things ought to be. Heidegger looked to a golden age.

Notice, the Romantic Movement was a struggle to come to terms with the darker side of modernity. Insofar as the Romantic Movement was animated by pangs of conscience with the machine, and all it represented to them, its adherents can be considered moralists. Paraphrasing William Blake, "How could they build their dark Satanic mills of England's green pastures?"[2]

Other questions follow: Where and when pastures were green? Can we ever get back to green pastures again? How do we not try?

---

2. Kunitz, *Essential Blake*, 60–61.

Acknowledgments

I wish to thank Peter McCormick, who at the time of drafting, was at the University of Liechtenstein. McCormick, with his combined interest in philosophy, literature, and twentieth-century European history, showed me philosophical vistas, which I longed to approach. Thanks to Barry Allen, of the Department of Philosophy at McMaster University, for his correspondence with me, which often buoyed me up in tough economic times, and to Anjan Chakravartty, of the Department of Philosophy at the University of Notre Dame, for helping me overcome my school boyishness, and have my say. I thank Jeff Sugarman, of the Faculty of Education at Simon Fraser University, where he specializes in counseling and educational psychology, with ongoing research into the socio-cultural dimensions of human agency; he continues to shape my thinking in subtle ways. For his continued support, thanks go out to Andrew Brook, the Chancellor's Professor of Philosophy and Cognitive Science at Carleton University.

Turning to where I have been earning my bread and butter, I am grateful to Dean Karen Roland, who has supported my research by allowing me to hang around in the Faculty of Education, at the University of Windsor, as well as my other colleagues here. I am thankful to the folks in the Department of Psychology, where I have been teaching and learning about what we do know about the self, however tentative and accumulating that is. Many other people assisted me in multifarious ways. With any undertaking of note, however, there are often doubters that hamper progress: I found a way around, or up and over, the roadblocks. Last but not least, it is probably bad form to thank oneself, but because of my persistence in the somewhat solitary pursuit that philosophy seems to lend itself to, I do.

Abbreviations

CORE WORKS

Heidegger

BP	*Basic Problems of Phenomenology* (originally published as *Die Grundprobleme der Phanomenologie*, 1927)
BT	*Being and Time* (originally published as *Sein und Zeit*, 1927)
CT	*The Concept of Time*
ER	*The Essence of Reasons* (originally published as *Vom Wesen des Grundes*, 1929)
H	*Heraclitus Seminar*
HCT	*History of the Concept of Time: Prologomena*
ID	*Identity and Difference* (originally published as *Identitat und Differenz*, 1959)
IM	*An Introduction to Metaphysics* (originally published as *Einfuhrung in die Metaphysics*, 1953)
KP	*Kant and the Problem of Metaphysics* (originally published as *Kant und das Problem der Metaphysic*, 1928)
LoH	"Letter on Humanism"
MFL	*Metaphysical Foundations of Logic* (originally published as *Metaphysische Anfangsgrunde der Logik im Ausgang von Leibniz*, 1928)
OWL	*On the Way to Language* (originally published as *Unterwegs zur Sprache*, 1959)
P	*Parmenides* (originally published as *Parmenides*, 1942–43)

PLT   Poetry, Language and Thought
PR   The Principle of Reason (originally published as *Der Satz vom Grund*, 1957)
QCT   The Question Concerning Technology
ST   Schelling's Treatise on the Essence of Human Freedom (originally published as *Schellings Abhandlung uber das Wesen der Menschlichen Friheit*, 1936)
TB   On Time and Being
WCT   What Is Called Thinking? (originally published as *Was Heisst Denken?* 1954)
WT   What Is a Thing?

ADDITIONAL WORKS

Hegel

EL   Encyclopedia of Logic with the Zusätze (originally published as *Encyklopädie der Philosophischen Wissenschaften. Tiel I Wissenshcaft der Logik*, 3rd ed., 1830)
PFA   Philosophy of the Fine Arts

Kant

CPJ   Critique of the Power of Judgement (originally published as *Critik der Urtheilskfaft*, 1790)
CPR   Critique of Practical Reason (originally published as *Kritik der Praktischen Vernunft*, 1788)
FMM   Foundations of the Metaphysics of Morals

Schweitzer

AU   Out of My Life and Thought: An Autobiography
PC   The Philosophy of Civilization
RL   Reverence for Life

ABBREVIATIONS

Other Authors

E   *Ethics* (Spinoza, originally published as *Ethica*, 1677).

PS   *Passions of the Soul* (Descartes, originally published as *Les Passions de L'âme*, 1649)

T   *Timaeus* (Plato)

Prologue
A Heideggerian Ethics and Yesterday

Existential philosophy is often thought to be concerned with existence. I shall question how far Heidegger succeeds in thinking about human life by looking to the domain of ethics. Just as we had knowledge before epistemology, we had some sort of ethics before we had philosophical treaties about it. I shall contend we must begin with how we are. To do otherwise is to be prey to what I will call the "unnatural fallacy," the idea we can prescribe an ethics derived from reason alone, putting our emotions, bodies, and socio-cultural histories, that is all the things that motivate us, in the back seat.

Heidegger claimed that ethics required that we have "beforehand succeeded in entering into a fundamental relationship with being."[1] What could a ethics founded on a relationship to being (*Bezug zum Seyn*) look like? We do not know because the cause has not been taken up, for reasons we can surmise. Like, such an ethics sounds obscure, which is no great benefit in the practical matters of living and dying.

Heideggerians concerned with ethics have tended to focus on Heidegger's early works, especially *Being and Time* in which, notoriously, there is scant attention to the being-question.[2] What ethical implications can be said to be consequent to Heidegger's work finds passing mention in Richardson's impressive study.[3] A recent commentator, Vogel concurs: Richardson, as part of the first wave of Heidegger scholars, had echoed the idea that an ethics can be developed from Heidegger's work.[4]

1. *IM*, 34.
2. *BT*, 149–68, 312–70.
3. Richardson, "Heidegger and Aristotle," 601.
4. Vogel, *Fragile We*, 88, 84.

More recently, Olafson, for example, offers a description of how human sociality can be explained by Heidegger's fundamental ontology[5] And Hodge has asked to what extent fundamental ontology is an ethics.[6] The intent of scholars has been to provide a modern day virtue ethics that becomes co-extensive with Heidegger's analytic of *Dasein* (his so-called "fundamental ontology"). The idea is that fundamental ontology is consistent with natural law inscribed in our nature. Vogel thinks, however, we need to supplement Heidegger's account of *Dasein* to make it immune from relativism.[7]

Some think, further, if there are any ethical implications of the later works, they are probably negative.[8] As Olafson points out, some have thought to concentrate on Heidegger's political views and not ethics.[9] The idea of a Heideggerian ethics has been compounded with his flirtation with Nazism. I comment upon Heidegger's Nazism, and how it bears upon the prospects for my project, in § 4.2.[10] Very little has been written, in any case, on how we ought to be related to being, or what that could even mean.[11] Further, scholars that have concentrated upon Heidegger's reading of the Greeks skirt around ethical implication of a relationship to being, often remaining timidly exegetical.[12] So looking to his later works as a basis of an ethics remains little remarked upon.

Previous commentators just do not follow Heidegger, in looking to the being-relationship (*Bezug zum Seyn*), as the basis of an ethics. A lot of exegetical work done on Heidegger has not interrogated his metaphysical commitments. Nor has Heidegger's critique of the history of Western philosophy been even attempted to be applied to ethics. Ethicists, furthermore, have overwhelmingly become disenchanted with the prospects for moral

---

5. Olafson, *Heidegger and the Ground of Ethics*, 13. Olafson rejected the idea that he is grounding ethics in human nature.

6. Hodge, *Heidegger and Ethics*, 189. Hodge correctly identified that Heidegger's critique does bear upon ethics, by showing that metaphysics was separated from ethics. She did not see, however, how the antipathy towards metaphysics parallels scepticism in the domain of ethics. She thought, rather, that overcoming metaphysics will have positive consequences for ethics.

7. Vogel, *Fragile We*, 1, 124.

8. Olafson, *Heidegger and the Ground of Ethics*, 98.

9. Ibid., 13–14.

10. Ibid.

11. Nicholson, *Illustrations of Being*.

12. Seidel, *Heidegger and the Pre-Socratics*.

realism, the notion there are some such things as moral truths for us to discover.

According to the moral realist, we can be right or wrong about what we think about ethics. Ethical knowledge, for the moral realist, at its base, represents truths about human nature (and about what human nature was meant to be). Moral realists have their defenders, modern day Aristotelians, Thomists, who defend natural law, and, of course, G. E. Moore's "metaphysical ethics."[13] Another notable moral realist is I. Murdoch.[14] We could develop or defend other moral realists, but those would be other books, not this one.

I need to say a word about dividing up Heidegger's work into the earlier and later (pre- and post-1927, respectively), which is commonplace in the literature. Though there is reason to divide up Heidegger's work, e.g., the later is different in focus and style, there is, I believe, a concern (the being-question) that Heidegger groped towards throughout his career. The texts I have chosen for study are based on their value to developing a Heideggerian ethic. I shall draw upon his later writings, starting in 1928 and most amply worked out after 1940, but not limit myself to them alone.

Also, a few preliminaries about the ethical enterprise are worth keeping in mind. I shall not distinguish between moralities and ethics; from a realist point-of-view, both have fallen into disrepute.[15] Ethics, so it is often claimed, is a matter of convention.[16] I shall assume that there are some moral fundamentals that are recognition transcendent; they are facts about human nature. I shall not spell out what those fundamentals are.

Richardson, part of the first wave of Heidegger scholarship in English, suggested that we must develop his thought in such a way as to pursue our own path.[17] The aim of this book is to develop a Heideggerian ethics as I envision it, as it may be useful to the current predicament of meta-ethics—how can values be intersubjectively constructed and objective?—and specifically to link the view I develop to the work of naturalists concerned about ethics.

I can anticipate in advance that my project of developing a Heideggerian ethics falls short because the lengths we have to go to make such

13. Moore, *Principia Ethica*, 110.

14. Murdoch, *Message to the Planet*.

15. Neilson *Ethics Without God*, 3; Searle, "How to Derive," 43–58; Singer, "Triviality of the Debate."

16. Mackie, *Cement of the Universe*; Stevenson, *Ethics and Language*; Williams, *Ethics*.

17. Richardson, "Heidegger and Aristotle," 628.

an account work becomes a lot to swallow. Why can we be ethical before having studied Heidegger? Had an experience of being, which we cannot articulate as obviously meaningful? Or had transpired any of the things Heidegger claims are necessary for Dasein to be in its right mind?

Still, and ironically, a Heideggerian ethics may count as an aesthetically pleasing way to think about our lives, shaped by fate. The irony lies that in an attempt to get back to basics, he has taken flight into the most distant. Because he engages, in a unique way to be sure, with the big themes of Western philosophy, the interest his writing garners has no easy antidote. This is especially true when we consider some of the alternatives that sometimes fail to resonate.

The upshot of the roadblocks I have encountered in developing Heidegger's ethics, however, is that we learn that we already find ourselves in a world where moral behavior is part of our tools for navigation. So the bypass is perhaps a happy one, I believe. We are once again, pointed to how the real world of sticks and stones, people and places, and words and worldviews intersect in our own lives that have a deep past and grow towards an uncertain but inevitable future. Ethics is a lot closer to us than being ever was, even if we sometimes think that what we do is a mark of something stupendous.

In part I, I focus on Heidegger's writings about ethics that could take us towards positive solutions to his being-question. There are, I shall argue in chapter 1, for example, positive links to metaphysics in Heidegger's thought, even though he is apt to use the term to denote the history of the forgetting of being. As with Aristotle there is no issue of more metaphysical import than being.[18] As Heidegger said, the being-question (*Seinsfrage*) "is quite simply the fundamental question of philosophy."[19] Even though Heidegger may talk of the "overcoming of metaphysics," his latter writings point us to a retrieval of a more original metaphysics, for which he turns our attention towards the pre-Socratics.[20]

---

18. As Aristotle tells us, philosophy is the science of being (*Metaphyiscs* 1060b30). And even though being has many senses, it is the task of philosophy to seek the first cause of a thing (ibid., 983a25). He wrote, "Therefore it is of being as being that we also must grasp the first causes" (ibid., 1003a30).

19. *MFL*, 136.

20. Wolin, *Heidegger Controversy*, 67.

Heidegger's later writings turn the focus away from *Dasein* and towards being.[21] In chapter 2, I attempt to explain Heidegger's contention that his ethics shall be consequent to having obtained a fundamental relationship to being.

In chapter 3, I consider Heidegger's reading of Kant, which is from the early period. Heidegger's reading of Kant, for instance, blurs the distinction between justification and motivation.

In chapter 4, I consider the romantic motivations behind Heidegger's program, and how this led him into two types of problems. First, National Socialism. Second, the idea that his philosophy is empty of sense. In this chapter, I will offer rejoinders to the dual challenge of Nazism and obscurantism.

In part II, chapters 5 and 6, I argue that is by way of mysticism that Heidegger can perhaps overcome his most difficult roadblock: what in the world is a being-relationship? I show how Heidegger, at least up to 1927, found it difficult to answer his own question about the meaning of being, and what he subsequently did to articulate it.

In part III, I consider various points of contrast and comparison to Heidegger. For example, in chapter 7, I consider Kant's ethical program. I shall explain how Heidegger can remedy some standard complains with Kant's ethics. In chapter 8, I look to Hegel's aesthetics to provide a hint about the nature of the experience of being—similar, perhaps to an aesthetic experience—to underpin Heidegger's ethics. In chapter 9, I consider Albert Schweitzer's metaphysical ethics, which I shall argue is an example of what a Heideggerian one could look like.

In chapter 10, I shall argue against moral relativism, suggesting further, that an environmental philosophy is perhaps consistent with a Heideggerian ethics.[22] In chapter 11, I consider neuroscience based evidence to support the idea of a realist ethics. In chapter 12, I provide conclusions about why ethics must precede metaphysics, namely, the fallout from this attempt to develop Heidegger's ethics. A fundamental relationship to being flows from or with, if it does at all, ethics.

---

21. Vogel, *Fragile We*, 1, 84, 88; Hodge, *Heidegger and Ethics*, 189; Olafson, *Heidegger and the Ground of Ethics*, 13, 96.

22. *BT*, 28.

PART I

Everyday Ethics

1

Ends and Origins

In reading the Pre-Socratics, Heidegger mediated upon the idea of *time*. I propose to use his discourse on time to begin to consider what a fundamental relationship to being could mean.

HOME

Heidegger tells us that to recover the inception of Western thought is a "new inception." To go back to the beginning is to reconfigure it in a new way. He explains, however, "Ground means being itself and this is the inception."[1] Being, according to Heidegger is the origin of the history of the West.

Heidegger dedicates much effort to tell us how not to relate to being, for example, conceiving of truth as adequate intuitive knowing.[2] He does not want to think of being in realist terms, for instance, as if it was mind-independent and our task is to grasp it. He tells us that Parmenides cannot be called a realist.[3] We cannot get into a fundamental relationship with being through any one sense. He explains:

> Of itself the soul extends itself out of itself towards being, i.e., it is the soul, purely by itself, that in the manner of [stretching itself out], understands anything like being.[4]

1. *CT*, 74.
2. *MFL*, 103.
3. Ibid., 142.
4. Ibid., 143.

Part I: Everyday Ethics

Yet we can wonder how a corporeal temporal object, like ourselves, can grasp ideas, which are seemingly nowhere, that is, perhaps outside of space and time. We can understand how I can pick up a table, but how do we relate to abstract objects? One answer is to refer to an analogy, namely, the notion that the eye can see the sun because it has something in common with it. Similarly, so the ancients sometimes held, the mind grasps ideas because it, too, shares something in common with them. The talk of likeness, of course, does not help, because it brings us to the famous mind-body problem. How does the body interact with the mind? It is somewhat self-evident, once again, how I can interact with a table, but how, specifically, does the brain relate to the mind? The same problem arises for our relationship for being. It is not at all clear how it would be possible to have relationship to being qua being.

The problem of cognitive access finds its crux in the notion of time. Heiedegger said that things have been thought to be (1) in time (nature and history), (2) outside time, and (3) above time. Being outside or above time is the non-temporal. Often God is said to be eternal, and thus by implication, perhaps outside or above time in some way and whatever that could mean. We could use "being" interchangeably with "God," since embracing a mystical element in Heidegger's thought, implies God in some form. Being is not a personal God in the Judeo-Christian tradition, who cares if we win the lottery or have a car accident. Being is far more abstract. Yet there is still the special relationship between being and humans that is within that tradition.

The problem of how an individual can hook on to being is transformed to overcome the chasm between the finite and infinite. Heidegger asks, "Our question is to what extent has a connection been seen between being and time."[5] The question, what is the meaning of being, becomes the problem, how can we relate to being other than temporally. That is to say, the best we can do, on Heidegger's account, is embrace the way that being opens itself up to us at any one time of history. Indeed, Heidegger himself, at the end of *Being and Time* asks if there is a way from primordial time to being?

The famous turn in Heidegger's thought is usually indexed to his attempts to purse the being-question, not to talk about it but to do it. He tells us that presentness (*Anwesneheit*) is related to being which is already

5. Ibid., 144.

"familiar" and given to us.[6] There is, he said, an understanding of being in the soul.[7] Yet the understanding is obviously not self-evident or we would not have forgotten the question of being in the first place.

Heidegger tells us that being includes four problems: (1) the problems of thinking of being as separate from particular beings (ontological difference); (2) of saying something about its truth character (the articulation of being); (3) that being is revealed to us differently in various time periods (veridical character of being); and (4) squaring the regionalism of being, while maintaining its unity overall (the unity of the idea of being).[8]

The four problems can be reduced to one. How can finite beings, like us, grasp being as such? How can we step outside of our historical time and place and view the origin of the entire history of humanity—how can we put ourselves into a fundamental relationship with being?

There is an important reason we must get back to a fundamental relationship with being: namely, it provides, according to Heidegger the spectre of freedom. He said that where there is freedom, there can be "for-the-sake-of."[9] Purpose. It is not just that we need freedom in order to intend to be concerned about this or that. More importantly, in the Western tradition, we need to have a freedom in order to comport ourselves properly as full human beings. We must have the freedom to be who we are, which, according to Heidegger, can only be properly arrived at when we have first put ourselves into a fundamental relationship with being.

Perhaps, one way around the problem of cognitive access is imagination. Could we imagine a relationship to being? Heidegger said, "Imagination, the intrinsic possibility of transcendence, is time, as primordial temporality."[10] So imagination cannot put us into a fundamental relationship with being; at best it can extend and amalgamate a world in which we already find ourselves. Imagination is finite, and as we have seen, being is anything but.

Heidegger's tack is to offer an original reading of Hereclitus and Parmenides. He tells us that Hereclitus and Parmenides were concerned with the eternal. What precedes and determines history, Heidegger said, is the beginning. He calls these Pre-Socratics (including also Anaximander)

---

6. Ibid., 145.
7. Ibid,, 148.
8. Ibid., 153.
9. Ibid., 185.
10. Ibid., 195.

primordial thinkers because they attempt to think the beginning. Being is the beginning.[11] It is easy to think that at the beginning of the temporal and changing world was something infinite. For onto-theologians, in the beginning was God.

The Pre-Socratics understood, for Heidegger, what philosophy was properly about, namely, the being-question, and developed a way of approaching it. Their style was poetic, often leaving us only fragments of verse. Yet Heidegger finds in these fragments more than in all the analysis Aristotle brings to any one topic. That we have 400 page books shows, said Heidegger, that "for a long time now the world has been out of joint and man is on a path of error."[12] Putting aside Heidegger's own choice of terms, he has a realist view of history; it is an objective fact that being has unfolded itself in the downward spiral leading to where we are, namely, according to Heidegger, homeless in the world.[13] To be out of sync with being therefore has ethical implications; we are not living the way we ought to be.

Heidegger tells us that the Roman conception of untruth, as *falsum* is what we work with in the nineteenth century, which is evidence, for him, of the decline of man. We think of being in terms of the truth and falsity of statements about particular beings, thus violating what Heidegger wants to do—think being qua being.

Heidegger's romanticism expressed itself in many ways that are telling. For instance, he wrote: "The typewriter tears writing from the essential realm of the hand, that is, the realm of the word."[14] Before the typewriter—and indeed before the word processor—we had, so he suggests, closeness to language that we have lost. Similarly, for Heidegger, before the world of the typewriter, speaking metaphorically, we apparently had a closer relationship to being. For Heidegger, it is not the typewriter, however, that is to fault, but something deeper, namely, the way, according to him, that we have become estranged from being. Being has become more deeply concealed from us than it previously was. It has withdrawn.[15]

Even though Heidegger has spoke of the end of philosophy, he saw it as crucially important. It is the philosopher that can acquaint herself with the unfolding of being. He said, therefore, "Men who lack philosophy are

---

11. *P*, 7.
12. Ibid., 8.
13. *MFL*, 56.
14. *P*, 80.
15. Ibid., 85.

without insight . . . They are at the mercy of the withdrawal and the concealment of being."[16] Philosophers that can recognize the withdrawal of being, may be able to put things right. We can perhaps reestablish a fundamental relationship with being, or at least document our demise.

What a fundamental relationship to being would amount to, of course, is obscure for some of the reasons already discussed—that is, it is not clear how we could interact with being qua being (discussed further in chapter 3). Let us turn our attention again to time.

Heidegger's question about the meaning of being is rhetorical. It is perhaps meant to goad us towards, what he calls, "thinking." Heidegger, nevertheless, tells us that being is the sole theme of philosophy, and he lays out ontological difference.[17] That is, we are supposed to distinguish being from particular beings; the former is supposed to precede particular things.[18] As he points out, however, what we could possibly say about being in general is obscure.[19] He claims that all the great philosophies since antiquity attempted to be ontology but failed.[20]

In *Basic Problems of Phenomenology*, Heidegger tells us that we interpret being by the way of time.[21] According to Heidegger, by interpreting the world temporally, we perceive being in a certain way that it makes itself present for us. He is not making the well-worn Platonic distinction between the changing world and an eternal one. Rather, his project is deeply rooted in the tradition of German Idealism. A key idea of German Idealism is that truth is manifest in history.

According to Heidegger, all of philosophy elucidates a world, which in itself is an expression of being. Heidegger regards the entire history of philosophy as the venue through which we access the way being has been given to us at that time in history.[22] By explaining how we have conceived of being, historically, he seeks to expose different ways in we have been configured as subjects.

Further, according to Heidegger, being has a destiny. An insipient idea in Heidegger's thought that there was a time when, let us suppose, as

16. Ibid., 120.
17. *BP*, 11, 78.
18. Ibid., 20.
19. Ibid., 13, 15.
20. Ibid., 12.
21. Ibid., 17.
22. Ibid., 23.

Part I: Everyday Ethics

Parmenades said, "being and thinking are the same." That is to say, there was a time, we can imagine, when we lived in accord with being; we had some direct access to the origin of everything. He seeks a retrieval (*Wiederholung*) of something that we have lost; namely, a relationship to being. The story of being is one of decline.

Heidegger warns us, however, "We wish to revive neither Aristotle nor the ontology of the Middle Ages, neither Kant nor Hegel, but only ourselves; that to say, we wish to emancipate ourselves from the phraseologies and conveniences of the present, which reels from one fashion to the next."[23] He tells us that retrieval cannot mean going back to the Greeks (though "retrieval" does suggest a looking back). We get at a hint of what he is aiming at when he contends that by pushing phenomenology to its limit has "the character of a setting free of the at-hand to let it be encountered."[24] Heidegger's entire philosophy can be summarized as an attempt to view what is present-at-hand (*Vorhanden*) into what is read-at-hand (*Zuhanden*). That is to say, he wished to expose the everyday basis of abstract concepts, like time (discussed further in chapter 5). However, Heidegger also thinks that the point of phenomenological reduction was to get at being: he did aim at some sort of original contact with being.[25]

Suffice it to say, for now, that though Heidegger did not want to revive any specific thinker in the past, he did want to appropriate the Pre-Socatics in order to construct a picture of the correct relationship to being.

To understand how the issue of time comes into play, in more detail, it is useful to provide some context concerning Heidegger's program. The story Heidegger tells could be called the withdrawal of being. According to Heidegger, at one time in our thinking, being was held together with *logos* and *physis*. The *logos* becomes the faculty that gathers together, yet in a way that externalises it as a force of nature. There was, in short, according to Heidegger, a unity of between nature, and us, where being pervaded both. Being revealed itself in a manner of nearness.

Heidegger, conversely, saw as revealing the separation and consequent reconfiguration of concepts, such as *logos* and *physis*. According to Heidegger, whereas *logos* was to be associated with thinking, being came to be construed as a thing. We came to wonder how ideas in the mind relate to things in the world. The world was out there; and we are stuck in our minds.

23. Ibid., 101.
24. Ibid., 118.
25. Ibid., 21.

Modern epistemology, for Heidegger, for instance, did not pose a problem to be solved, but rather was symptomatic of a malady, that is, the forgetting of being.

According to Heidegger, other consequences of our forgetting of being are the dichotomies between, on the one hand, essence and appearance, and on the other, being and becoming. We come to take ideas as eternal and pit them against appearances that are fleeting. He attacks a metaphysical realist conception of knowledge, which depends upon a correspondence theory of truth: the notion that there are mind-independent truths that we hope to mirror.

For Heidegger, the dichotomy between objects and representational thinking, however, is also the basis for the separation of metaphysics from ethics rooted in a further set of distinctions: is from ought, facts from values, and the theoretical from the practical.[26] According to him, we have come to view being as a theoretical and objective matter divorced from an ethic that comes to be construed in terms of subject preference. That is, where correspondence fails, often first for instance, in the domain of ethics and aesthetics, the result is subjectivism. Instead of arguing against the subjectivism or objectivism of values, he critiqued the way the issues are consequent to a certain understanding of truth, and more generally, the way being is disclosed to us.

Heidegger is critical of the history of philosophy after the Pre-Socratics. Since, according to him, things are getting worse—being continues to withdraw. Similarly, Heidegger is critical of the notion of truth as the property of a proposition, which he took to be symptomatic of a stage in the decline of being.[27] He tells us that for the Greeks, for instance, truth means "to take out of concealment uncovering, unveiling."[28] He went on, "To be sure the Greek interpretation of this phenomenon was not successful in every respect."[29]

Heidegger, at any rate, said that truth is "for-us."[30] Truth is the way being is disclosed to us, which included the way we conceive of all our basic concepts (like truth). Knowledge, he told us, requires an understanding we

---

26. *LoH*, 259.
27. *BP*, 201.
28. Ibid., 215.
29. Ibid.
30. Ibid., 221.

Part I: Everyday Ethics

have projected.[31] The idea of "for-us" sounds idealistic. Heidegger wished to avoid talk of idealism and realism (since such talk also indicates the forgetting of being).

AMBIGUITY

McCormick remarked that Heidegger's attitude towards metaphysical reflection is obscure.[32] Nicholson, some years later, took the next step when he asks, "What, then, is the import of this positive link between Heidegger and metaphysics?[33] Hodge concedes, more recently, "The critique of metaphysics does not lead to an erasure of metaphysics."[34] Insofar as anyone has considered the relationship between metaphysics and ethics in Heidegger's thought, we can turn to the words of Hodge: "I suggest that Heidegger did not celebrate an already achieved overcoming of metaphysics but diagnosed a need for such an overcoming, if human beings are to flourish."[35] Though there is ambiguity in Heidegger's position.

We have the following themes in Heidegger's writings:

1. The question of being.
2. Evading realism-idealism debates, symptomatic of the withdrawal of being, and returning to the concrete practices upon which these abstract debates depend.
3. We can, by reading ancient texts, retrieve something that has been lost in the history of the west, a fundamental relationship to being.

The first and third points are metaphysical, in the traditional sense that they are concerned with our relationship to an ultimate reality. The anti-metaphysical strain comes with the second point, dealing with Heidegger's deconstruction of the history of Western ontology.

The ambiguity in Heidegger's thought comes from wondering if, say like the later Wittgenstein, he wants to do away with metaphysical questions and happily abide in the finite and conventional world he finds himself. Or are we to read Heidegger as a mystic as he looks to the to the Pre-Socratics,

---

31. Ibid., 284.
32. McCormick, *Heidegger*, xix.
33. Nicholson, *Illustrations of Being*, xi.
34. Hodge, *Heidegger and Ethics*, 31.
35. Ibid., 12.

and comments on poets, like Hölderlin, to achieve a poetic method of doing philosophy.

To understand how we could have a fundamental relationship to being, it is edifying to see what Heidegger took from his reading of Heraclitus and Parmenides. Usually, these two figures are juxtaposed. For Heraclitus everything is changing, and for Parmenides an unchanging world is set beside one that is in flux. Heidegger contends, however, that they were saying the same things. That is, Heidegger tried to think being and becoming as the same thing. What is eternal is present in what is changing. Being is manifest in the history of the world, which has a destiny (*Geshik*).

Notice, if primordial time and being are the same thing, the problem of cognitive access evaporates. There is a reason, furthermore, to think, for Heidegger, that primordial time and being can be co-extensive. It is the retrieval of a mythical Greece that Heidegger beckons us to because that is when he thinks that being had not withdrawn from the horizon of the West. It is precisely in the *mythos* of ancient Greece that Heidegger seeks to retrieve, even if that merely sets the model of what he aims at today. For all the talk of destroying the history of Western onto-theology, Heidegger seeks a union with being.

To take Heidegger seriously, means we accept that human nature finds fulfillment in a fundamental relationship with being in such a way that is beneficial for ourselves and our relations to others. In the next chapter, I want to explore, in greater detail, the being-relationship by considering in more detail Heidegger's later writings related to the Pre-Socratics.

2

Ethical Thinking

A Heideggerian ethic can perhaps be likened best to an orientation towards the world, which results in a feeling. We begin with what Heidegger has to say about thinking, because on his account it is part and parcel of the modern, now controversial separation of cognitive and affective processes in psychology.

THINKING

Heidegger talks much more in the later work about thinking than feeling. By thinking, he did not mean the ability to reason. Calculative thinking is, after all, the object of his critique in *The Question Concerning Technology*. Nor can thinking be intuitive if that is implicated in a correspondence, and hence, representational theory of truth.

At best, Heidegger left us with figurative turns of phrase to explain himself. Thinking, for Heidegger, has a kinship to asking questions. To think is to pursue a path. More precisely, it is to be on a path. The difference between pursuing a path and being on one has to do with the way in which the will recedes into the background when we are on a path. Just as we do not construct a world, but find ourselves in one, so too, according to Heidegger, does the thinker find oneself on a path.

It is important to emphasize the submissive nature of being on a path. The idea of submissiveness, in fact, punctuates many of Heidegger's

Ethical Thinking

comments. He tells us that a teacher must allow student "to let learn."[1] He has in mind not the conveying of information from one to another, but rather an allowing something that is already insipient within the student come to light.

His notion of thinking also bears the hallmarks of submissiveness. He tells us that thinking and gathering are all that concern him.[2] He aspired to a sort of thinking that is "thankful" that "would dwell in memory . . . originary expression."[3] We are thankful when we receive something. Heideggerian thinking is a retrieval of something already given but now forgotten.

The forgetting of the question of being, for Heidegger, marks a reconfiguration of what we mean when we say we think. The forgetting of being marks the "decline of the West" (words made famous by Spengler's book of the same title). Heidegger tells us that Spengler's words are a consequence of Nietzsche's: "The wasteland grows."[4] Heidegger comments, "The one true words."[5] Yet he also tells us that darkening has nothing to do with the decline and fall of the West.[6] For Heidegger, darkening has everything to do with the assent of the West, insofar as it represents technological thinking reaching its climax.

As we have seen, Heidegger's solution to the problem of our loss of an ideal relationship to being is ambiguous. He looks to the Pre-Socratics but reassured us that we cannot go back. As he puts it, "We are too late for the gods and too early for Being."[7] Nonetheless, seeing that he maintains that the origin of something is the source of its nature, it is plausible to think that to properly become what we are, we must be in touch with our source—being.[8]

One way that Heidegger attempts to articulate a fundamental relationship to being is by an extended mediation on works of art. Incidentally, he tells us that the history of Western art corresponds with the change in the nature of truth. We ask about the objectivity of an evaluation of an

---

1. *WCT*, 15.
2. Ibid., 147.
3. Ibid.
4. Ibid., 38.
5. Ibid., 180.
6. Ibid.
7. *PLT*, 4.
8. Ibid., 17.

artwork.[9] We can, at any rate, at least imagine what it would mean to use a work of art to express, first, a world, and second, as a means to decipher the way in which being is being articulated.

Heidegger had dwelt upon the poetry of Hölderlin. Heidegger valued Hölderlin because he views him as a poet of a "destitute time."[10] Of course there are many post-World War II poets that could be used to articulate the agony of the death camps, like O. E. Mandelstam, for instance. The destitution that Heidegger saw is not as concrete as the lack of affordable housing. The homelessness he discussed has to do with being abandoned spiritually. "Not only have the gods and the god fled, but the divine radiance has become extinguished in the world's history."[11] Our separation from being is a "default."[12] For Heidegger, "Hölderlin is the precursor of poets of a destitute time."[13] Hölderlin expressed not only the loss, but the hoped for retrieval. Heidegger praises, for instance Schelling's treatise on human freedom because he detects in it the fundamental mood of Hölderlin.[14]

In fact, the fundamental relationship to being is to lead to something very close to a mood, which is given to us. The idea of what is given is important. For instance, Heidegger said, "But origin always comes to meet us from the future."[15] The future, for Heidegger, is, in some sense, part of the destiny of being; it is given to us. We receive it; he calls this experience of acceptance "submission."[16] We must be in a submissive mood. We accept, receive, thankfully, submit.

The submission theme, in relation to being, is present in Heidegger's essay, "Letter on Humanism" in a startling, though in his typical style. He tells us that thinking lets itself be "claimed" by being.[17] The entire idea of submission, admittedly, rings poorly in our ears unethical; since the enlightenment freedom is often taken to be the foundation of ethics, for example, in Kant's writing the will is what gives us dignity. If we cannot make

---

9. Ibid., 81.
10. Ibid., 91.
11. Ibid.
12. Ibid.
13. Ibid., 142.
14. *ST*, 164.
15. *OWL*, 10.
16. Ibid., 57.
17. *LoH*, 218.

Ethical Thinking

a choice then the question of ethics does not arise; we are neither, for Kant, moral agents or patients.

Heidegger confirms the discord between a fundamental relationship to being and ethics, when he said that when original thinking ends, ethics arises.[18] Thus, a fundamental relationship to being may be antithetical to what we usually call "ethics."

Yet not everything Heidegger said about ethics is disparaging either. He tells us that the tragedies of Sophocles preserved *ēthos* more primordially than Aristotle's lectures on ethics. It cannot be long treatise, heavy with argument, that convey a fundamental relationship to being—the ethical life—but rather art, poetry, and perhaps above all, in the Heideggerian sense, thinking.

So we are advised to be cautious about interpreting his disparaging remarks about ethics. It is fair to say that Heidegger will be critical of the modern approach to ethics, insofar as it is tied to notion of truth, the subjectivity of values and a representational theory of truth, which he criticizes.

For Heidegger, all humanisms are grounded in some metaphysics.[19] In order to go beyond metaphysics, that is, the history of the forgetting of being, Heidegger employs, once again, language that is highly figurative. He tells us that man is the shepherd of being.[20] The vocation of shepherd here implies that we have some special relationship to being. The inference the analogy indicates is obvious: Man without being, is like a shepherd without his flock—lost.

HEDEGGERIAN ETHICS

Hiedegger's concept of thinking, as we already intimated, has mystical overtones. Caputo tried to emphasize that his book on this topic was intended to highlight a mystical element in Heidegger's thought.[21] As Caputo pointed out, nonetheless, we may worry that mysticism, which requires dissolution of the self, puts us beyond ethics.[22] Yet he went on, "Heidegger's

---

18. OWL, 219.
19. Ibid., 225.
20. Ibid., 234.
21. Caputo, *Mystical Element*, xvii.
22. Ibid., 44.

position should not be criticized for failing to be what it was never intended to be—viz., metaphysical ethics—which is what is usually done."[23]

To the claim that Heidegger never intended a metaphysical ethics, I remain somewhat indifferent, since I have already said, in the prologue, that I am extending his work. At the same time, we may hope that Caputo may be sympathetic to my attempt to draw out a metaphysical ethics from Heidegger, as he tells us that we must do more than interpret Heidegger.[24]

There are a handful of people who attempt to extend Heidegger's thought on ethics, along the lines I have in mind, namely, metaphysically; and it is worthwhile to consider how their writings could go in this direction, even if that is not what they intended. Caputo also recognized how Heidegger's critique of subjectivity bears on ethics, yet said, "But it was not Heidegger's intention to cut himself off from every possible ethics, but rather to put in the place of the impoverished ethics of values a deeper thinking of the originary *ethos*."[25] As Caputo puts it:

> Talk about the truth of being is ethical talk of a more, radical originary sort... So it is a serious mistake to think that Heidegger has no ethics, and a serious underestimation of his work if we fail to take into account the salutary routing and deconstruction of value-thinking that occurs in his thinking... For if Heidegger displaces metaphysical ethics, he does so by putting an originary ethics in its place.[26]

Caputo attempts to suggest what an originary ethics would look like, for which he looks to Meister Eckhart and the notion of letting-be (*Gelassenheit*). Caputo wrote:

> *Gelassenheit* meant letting God be God, letting him be—in yourself, in others, in everything... That is why in Meister Eckhart *Gelassenheit*, letting-be, was a principle of love (*caritas*).[27]

Caputo concludes:

> Although I cannot spell it out here, I think that a good deal of what Heidegger is up to is found in the notion of *Gelassenheit* as

---

23. Ibid., 256.
24. Ibid., 270.
25. Ibid., 55.
26. Ibid., 56.
27. Ibid., 61.

"openness to the mystery," as a deep respect for the world, for others, for the gods.[28]

Caputo's tack resonated with B. J. Boelen's idea of 1968, in looking for the ground of ethics in an orientation towards the world. In Boelen's paper, "The Question of Ethics in Heidegger's Thought" begins with the author tracing Heidegger's critique of the subjectivity of value, and proposing that an ethic of loving should supplement Heidegger's talk of thinking and dwelling in the house of being.[29] Love is a feeling and entails an orientation towards the beloved.

A Heideggerian ethics amounts to letting beings be. Consistent with the key notion of submission, we should let things be what they are. The philosophy that most comes to mind here is ancient Chinese Taoism. (Heidegger attempted once to comment on the *Tao Te Ching*, with little success.) One ideal in Taoism is the uncarved block. Like an uncarved block we should be as we are; the way nature made us. Not only should we let beings be, but also let ourselves be. By letting ourselves be, we can infer, is the deepest expression of having a fundamental relationship with being.

There are two worries with such a declaration as "letting beings be," and it is helped little by looking to Taoism. First, letting things be is counterintuitive. What makes us human is that we can shape our nature. We live in houses, drive cars, and do all sorts of things which require us to change the way things are. Specifically, if we were just to "let things be," how would it be possible to develop as human beings? The romantic freedom of letting things be flies in the face of human culture, which, in part, shapes what we are.

The following maxim is handy, however: Freedom without culture is barbarism, and culture without freedom is tyranny. That is to say, we need to have some social influence in order to develop, yet it cannot be so constraining as to suffocate individual freedom. Thus, letting things be, for human beings, must mean, if it is to be plausible, letting nature take its course, which includes some socio-cultural impositions.

Second, Heidegger gave us no specific advice on how to deal with specific ethical problems. Is he for or against the death penalty? Yet as I have already hinted at in the prologue, a Heideggerian ethics operates at the level of the general ground of ethics, being concerned with motivation, not what is good in this or that case. The orientation of submission that a

---

28. Ibid., 62.
29. Frings, *Heidegger*.

fundamental relationship to being entails, for Heidegger, leads to the ethic of letting things be. Helping them, at the most, to be what they are intended to be.

The idea of letting things be, nevertheless, is still hopelessly vague. That is, even at the level of motivation, a Heideggerian letting beings be could support the ethic of Mother Teresa or other more unsavory figures. It could be interpreted in ways that are wide and varied, to a point of uselessness.

Perhaps reminding ourselves of how far lifeboat ethics has taken us will lower our standards from what we expect from ethics in terms of particular judgements. Analytic ethics does not, at any rate, offer a clear justification for the values we adhere to. Worse, the failure to provide a justification for core values has led in some quarters to subjectivism-cum-relativism (discussed further in chapter 6).

Nevertheless, criticizing applied ethics is not going to render the vagueness of a Heideggerian ethics innocuous; that is, even if we lower our expectations from the discipline of ethics, not requiring universal judgements about particular acts (say, along the lines of the generalizations we find in Aristotle's ethics of virtue), we still demand something more than a warm and fuzzy feeling about being. Needless to say, we need to say more than a bit more about what a relationship to being could mean for ethics. In the next chapter, I shall consider Heidegger's original reading of Kant, specifically, how a feeling could serve as the foundation of ethics.

3

Back to Before Kant

A lecture course Heidegger gave in 1927, and published as *The Basic Problems of Phenomenology* is rarely identified as a source for his ethics. Generally, the lack of attention given by previous commentators to *The Basic Problem of Phenomenology*, in this context, is glaring because it contains a highly original interpretation of Kant's ethical program, and I shall argue, can set the tone for Heidegger's own.

I shall first consider Heidegger's reading of Kant's ethical program. Second, I consider what Heidegger took from his original reading of Kant: specifically, I shall argue that we can read him as seeking the justification of ethics in an epiphany.

KANTIAN ETHICS

According to Heidegger, Kant's entire ethics rests on respect (*Achtung*) between moral agents. Kant calls respect a "feeling" that provides the motivation for the ethical law, which is produced by reason itself.[1] Heidegger wrote of Kant's ethics, "Respect is the mode of the ego's being-with-itself."[2] Heidegger comments:

> That Kant gives the answer in the ontology of human existence, or the metaphysics of morals, shows that he has an unclouded

1. BP, 133–35.
2. Ibid., 134.

> understanding of the methodological sense of the analysis of the person thus also of the metaphysical question, What is man? Let us once again make clear to ourselves what is inherent in moral feeling: man's dignity, which exalts him insofar as he serves. In this dignity in unity with service, man is at once master and servant of himself. In respect, in acting ethically, man makes himself.[3]

Ethics cannot, for Heidegger, be about a statement being right or wrong, but rather, human nature. Heidegger claims that Kant's groundwork in the first Critique sets the basis for an anthropology.[4] Heidegger conjectures, for instance, "Perhaps it is precisely time which is the *a priori* of the ego—time, to be sure, in a more original sense then Kant was able to conceive it."[5] As with Aristotle, Heidegger is interested in what sort of person we can become. Throughout Heidegger's reading, we encounter Kant elucidating a theory of human nature, too.[6]

According to Heidegger's reading, for Kant, "Respect means responsibility towards oneself and this in turn means being free. Being free is not a property of man but is synonymous with behaving ethically."[7] When we respect ourselves, that is, achieve our end, we are free and ethical.[8]

Arguably, then, Kant articulated the Christian notion "thy will shall be done on earth as it is in heaven." The collective satisfaction of all of our natures is the Kantian kingdom of ends. Heidegger contends the Kantian kingdom of ends is ontic: "being-with-one-another."[9] The kingdom of ends is the place where all people achieve their particular end in a manner that does not harm others.

The Kantian idea that man should always be an end unto himself takes on a new emphasis in Heidegger's thought.[10] That is, it is not only that we ought not to be means to ends, but rather that we have a collective *telos*.

For Heidegger, the focus shifts away from the Kantian formalism of the categorical imperative, towards an analytical of Dasein.[11] For instance, Hei-

---

3. Ibid., 137.
4. *KP*, 144, 147.
5. *BP*, 145.
6. Ibid., 136.
7. Ibid., 141.
8. Ibid., 169.
9. Ibid., 139.
10. Ibid., 138.
11. *KP*, 50.

degger wonders, "Now to what extent does [Kantian] respect correspond to the essential structure of feelings and why is it pure feeling."[12] Heidegger frames things in a manner consistent with his fundamental ontology (e.g., his analysis of moods in *Being and Time*).

TRAJECTORY

Schalow, in a detailed study, *The Renewal of the Heidegger-Kant Dialogue: Action, Thought, and Responsibility*, is useful in explaining how Heidegger's reading of Kant potentially contributes towards an ethics. As Schalow points out, for instance, Heidegger downplays Kant's distinction between duty and inclination.[13] In other words, what feelings motivate one to act ethically could serve a role in justifying duty that cannot be derived by reason alone. So what sort of feeling are we on about?

Schalow says, "[T]he claims of moral responsibility (as seen in respect) must be shown to derive from human finitude in such a way that practical reason itself can be revealed to be inherently temporal."[14] That is to say, Heidegger looked for a way to ground ethics in the world.

Heidegger hoped to recast, as Schalow explains, human freedom in a way not opposed to nature.[15] We may wish to recall that for Kant, we are not determined to do an act, in the way that billiard balls will follow a certain trajectory when hit a certain way. Schalow explains, "That is, freedom must be seen to arise from a will which not only stems from human nature, but as such can empower or enable us to become engaged in precisely those concerns which determine the 'highest ends' of our humanity."[16] The goal, according to Heidegger's reading of Kant, is to show how freedom is the end of human nature.[17] Freedom must be understood not only as a will to choose but also to become a particular sort of entity.

Kant's account of ethics harkens us to what is outside of time, namely, God, freedom, and immortality. Further, ethical judgements are to be universal and thus also free from the corruption of time. Conversely, what is in time, such as nature is antithetical to ethics. For Heidegger, the temporal

---

12. *BP*, 110.
13. Schalow, *Imagination and Existence*, 274.
14. Ibid., 277.
15. Ibid., 290, 389.
16. Ibid., 295.
17. Ibid., 296.

must be included in the foundation of ethics. In a nutshell, Heidegger, by rendering ethics contingent upon an experience of nature, includes time at the basis of ethics.

To become a particular sort of entity requires, for Heidegger an experience of nature. That is, talk of God, we could say for the purpose of exposition, is transformed into discussions of the disclosure of being, for which he looks to the pre-Socratics' notion of nature (*physis*).

Thus, an experience of nature, as conceived by Heidegger's reading of the pre-Socratics, is required to motivate a Heideggerian ethics. More specifically, the affect of an original encounter with nature, according to Schalow, and the thrust of Heidegger's exchange with Kant, is so that we can explicitly engage in letting beings be.[18] Since nature may be finite, Heidegger can claim to avoid a Platonist metaphysics, by grounding ethics in the temporal world. The talk of finitude becomes our experience, according to Heidegger, of an eternal presence.[19]

The ambiguity of Heidegger's approach towards being is betrayed in how he deals with the philosophical problem of the nature of time. He distinguishes, for instance, between historical time and original time.[20] In the early works, original time, to be sure, is the one we use so we are not late for lunch.[21] Time conceived of in terms of the prime characteristic of *Dasien*, and hence in terms of finitude.[22] The notion of original time as being inculcated in practices, however, took on a greater metaphysical air as his writings develop. As he said, even early on, "It is not possible to go into further detail here on the finitude of time, because it is connected with the difficult problem of death."[23]

Death threatens his goal to think Dasein in radically finite ways.[24] If death is to be taken to indicate the unknown, it has perhaps the same place in Kant's thinking as the thing-in-itself: the hereafter, which is said to be eternal, is an object of faith. Heidegger finds the idea, however, of the infinite difficult, complaining that Kant cannot distinguish between higher and

---

18. Ibid., 302, 383. Schalow conjectured, further, that making ethics dependent on nature may extend our circle of concern beyond humans.
19. Ibid., 388, 397.
20. *BP,* 231.
21. Ibid., 260.
22. Ibid., 271–72.
23. *BP,* 273.
24. *KP,* 161.

lower infinites, because both rest on the sensible.[25] Perhaps just as Heidegger wants to bring us to practices, he expects Kant to remain within the sensible world he circumscribed in the first critique. As already indicated, however, Heidegger, with death, potentially acknowledged something that goes well beyond finitude.

To get a sense of what Heidegger's account of time amounts to in the end, we need to look the role it plays in human development both psychologically and historically. Heidegger tells us, "If authentic existence, resoluteness, is grounded in a specific mode of temporality, then a specific present belongs to resoluteness."[26] That is to say, if authentic being depends upon a specific mode of temporality, then that is necessary in order to be ethical. We must understand mode in terms of a manner of being. A manner of temporality can be usefully rephrased as "a way of being towards time." He thinks that if temporality is the basis for Dasein, then so too, is temporality the basis of the question of being.[27]

As he noted, understanding being through time is a radicalization of a repetition of the problems of ancient philosophy.[28] The sort of time Heidegger focuses upon, and which is of interest to us, is the instant (*Augenblick*). He is quick to reassure us that the instant is not that abstract moment of derivative time, but somehow related to temporality, that is, the conditions for Dasein's possibilities.[29]

For Heidegger, there is a union of thought and being in the following sense: the history of ideas is co-extensive with the record of the way being has been disclosed to us. Yet for Heidegger mysticism cannot lie in contending that the history of being is co-extensive with, what we can call roughly, the intellectual history of humanity (especially in the West, beginning in ancient Greece, where we supposedly abided with being in a more primary way). Still, Heidegger adopts a mystical type of language; he claims, for instance, that Hegel was on the right track by saying that being and nothing are identical.[30] So Heidegger aims, by turning to the Pre-Socratics and the poems of Hölerlin, towards articulating a moment of vision when being will be present.

25. *KP*, 102.
26. *BP*, 287.
27. *KP*, 168.
28. *BP*, 316.
29. Ibid., 287–88.
30. Ibid., 312.

Part I: Everyday Ethics

In the twentieth century, philosophers, and at least since Kant, have rightly busied themselves with coming to terms with modern science. Along with modern science came humanism, the displacement of religion, and an attempt to overcome every obstacle technologically. Following suit, the goal of modern philosophy, stylistically, perhaps emulating the sciences, was to be clear and distinct. So it is little surprise that modern accounts of ethics tend to seek out some type of formal rules where we can, sometimes literally in the case of Bentham, make use of a calculus to determine what we should do. But for Heidegger, modern science is part of the history of the forgetting of being. His entire approach to ethics cuts against the modern tradition.

Of this we can be sure. What adherents of various philosophical camps have much less to say about, and what Heidegger dwells up almost exclusively in his pithy assertions about ethics, is why one should be ethical in the first place. Why engage in the thought experiment of the categorical imperative? Why act to maximize a utility for everyone? At a Heideggerian level of generality, where getting up close and personal with being serves to motivate an ethics, there is little difference between Kantians and utilitarians; both are trying to formalize the practice of ethics according to certain rules, perhaps with some emendations to practice.

It is worthwhile, thus, to acknowledge this. What we may get with a Heideggerian ethics is a justification of what could motivate one, with less detail about what to do in any one situation. And that is not entirely a bad thing; given the failure to ground ethics has loomed large over modern accounts.

Taking our cue from Heidegger's reading of Kant, the motivation to be ethical rests, at least ideally, in an experience of nature. With all of the provisos made plain about what we should not expect, there could be still some picture we could paint of what sort of life would be consistent with a Heideggerian ethics, and what not (discussed further in chapter 8).

Yet before attempting to add detail to a Heideggerian ethic, I need to address some of the generic criticisms that Heidegger just has nothing to say about ethics. The level of generality of a Heideggerian account is too broad to be interesting. Further, detractors often abhor his writing style, which they find vacuous; are fixed upon his flirtation with Nazism; and on occasion detect substantial problems related to the consistency of his position. We turn to these matters next.

4

Romanticism Revisited

Heidegger's political romanticism has made him the object of philosophical critiques related to his membership in the Nazi party. Also, Heidegger's penchant for lyrical effusions, and panache for executing them, in his latter writings, has led Edwards, in Heidegger's *Confusions*, to take aim at ambiguities. According to Edwards, Heidegger's Nazism is the inevitable outcome of muddled thinking.

First, I take up the challenge of confronting the dark side of romanticism, in this context, Nazism and obscurantism. Second, I look to some of the poets "of a destitute time" that influenced Heidegger's thought. Finally, I consider Heidegger as romantic in the tradition of Oswald Spengler's *Decline of the West*, as well as the psychologist, Abraham Maslow's account of peak experiences.

THE CHARGE OF NAZISM

Farías' groundbreaking work, *Heidegger and Nazism*, made it difficult to minimize Heidegger's politics. Farías wrote: "My central thesis is the following: When Heidegger decided to join the National Socialist Party, he was following an already-prepared path whose beginnings we find in the Austrian movement of Christian Socialism, with its conservativism and anti-Semitism, and in the attitudes he had found in his native region (Messkrich and Konstanz), where he began his studies."[1]

---

1. Farías, *Heidegger and Nazism*, 4.

Part I: Everyday Ethics

Farías adds, "The Christian Socialist movement came from Catholic romantic sources, and, like romanticism, viewed the Enlightenment as its chief enemy."[2] Romantics often pinned for the safety of regional hamlets, politically often expressed as a desire for a homeland (*Heimat*).[3]

On May 1, 1933 Heidegger joined the NSDAP. On the May 27, 1933, at the even of the ceremonial transfer of the rector's office, he gave the now infamous speech, "The Self-Determination of the German University." This speech is much quoted, yet I shall still reproduce some relevant passages. Heidegger wrote:

> The German university is valued by us as the loftiest school that educates the leaders and the guards of the fate of the German nation through and from the power of science. To will the essence of the German university is to will that science to be informed by the historical spiritual mission of the German people.[4]

He went on:

> However, the beginning (*Angung*) has not been overcome or reduced to nothing. For, provided that the original Greek science is something great, the *beginning* (*Angung*) of this greatness remains its *greatest* quality . . . The beginning remains us. It does not lie *behind* us as the past that is long gone, but it is still *before* us. As the greatest, the beginning will outlast everything that is to come. It will discard us as well. The beginning has penetrated to our own future; it is standing there over us as the distant degree, instructing us to recover its greatness once again . . . But if we submit ourselves to the distant call of the beginning, then science must become the basic event of our spiritual-national existence.[5]

Heidegger's romanticism expressed itself in a desire to commune with his ancestry and native land.[6]

The danger in analyzing someone's work in retrospect, however, is that we can engage in rational reconstruction. If someone had gone on a killing spree, we may interpret that person's every gesture (say they were quiet) as evidence something was askew. The same evidence, being quiet, however, could be interpreted differently if they had won say, the Victoria Cross.

2. Ibid., 27.
3. Ibid., 91.
4. As cited in ibid., 99.
5. As cited in ibid., 101.
6. Ott, *Martin Heidegger*, 47.

Farías warns, "In no sense can we read National Socialism into *Being and Time,* but we can identify philosophical beliefs that foreshadow Heidegger's latter convictions."[7]

Tom Rockmore, in *On Heidegger's Nazism and Philosophy,* points out that it is important to understand what Nazism meant to Heidegger.[8] Rockmore points out that Heidegger supported a redress from World War I, specifically the Treaty of Versailles. He also wanted to see the historical realization of the German folk (*Volk*).[9] Safranski offers a useful summary of grievances, in his biographical study, noting Heidegger supported unilateral repudiation of (1) The Treaty of Versailles; (2) withdrawal from the League of Nations; and (3) annexation of lands (as Germans lived beyond German borders).[10]

Heidegger embraced the romantic nationalism that motivated Nazism. Ironically, Heidegger also thought Nazism was opposed to technology, illustrating the extent to which he focused in on the romantic ideal of a return to an idyllic homeland.

To be sure, when convenient, Heidegger also embraced anti-Semitism. When he wanted someone to be dismissed from their job, Heidegger was anti-Semitic. When he had an affair with Hannah Arendt, a Jew, he was not. Nor was he anti-Semitic insofar as he often assisted Jewish students with their research. He was not consistent in his anti-Semitism, as is already well known.

He was anti-Semitic as an effect of a type of German nationalism (which required the exclusion of the non-German folk). It is doubtful, however, that Heidegger endorsed the final solution, that is, a eugenics program that entailed the systematic extermination of European Jewry. Though he did little to protest the mass murder of the Jews (and others), he at no time endorsed it. As Safranski points out, Heidegger was not anti-Semitic in the Nazi sense.[11] As part of the de-Nazification hearings, Heidegger wrote the chairman of the commission on December 15, 1945. Heidegger pointed out that he indeed supported the national and social component of Nazism but not the "ideological doctrine of biological radicalism."[12]

---

7. Farías, *Heidegger and Nazism,* 60.
8. Rockmore, *On Heidegger's,* 285.
9. Ibid., 35.
10. Safranski, *Martin Heidegger,* 293.
11. Ibid., 254.
12. As cited in Ott, *Martin Heidegger,* 333.

Part I: Everyday Ethics

Ott, another of Heidegger's biographers, who focused on the political element, explains the bizarre reasons for which Heidegger rejected Nazism. Ott contends that Heidegger rejects Nazism "for its supposed failure to provide an adequate theory of Being."

Rockmore's analysis, however, is more pessimistic than many previous commentators. He thinks that Heidegger's Nazism did follow from his philosophy.[13] According to Rockmore, it makes little sense to say Heidegger is a great thinker who failed to confront Nazism.[14] Heidegger's Nazism indicates errors in his philosophy.

Yet to claim that Heidegger's fundamental ontology is the basis for his Nazism requires explaining precisely how. On their own, Heidegger's romanticism, critique of technology, nationalism, and his fundamental ontology, does not entail Nazism. Logically, we could not infer one doctrine (Nazism) from the others (either individually or collectively).

Romanticism, notice, can move in two directions. Anarchists and communists share many of the same frustrations that Heidegger did about the effects of industrialization, urbanization, and what was entailed in rationalization of the world, when it destroyed community. Yet anarchists rejected the state as a vehicle for liberation, and rather emphasized individual liberty.

Conversely, fascists demanded that authority, as expressed in the hyper-nationalism of Nazi rhetoric, glorified the state's role to protect the folk, and more importantly, for Heidegger, the German spirit (*Deutch-Geist*). Heidegger was a fascist.

Heidegger's fascism, though disgusting, was not full-blown Nazism, which requires a commitment to: (1) German nationalism, (2) anti-Semitism, and (3) the holocaust. Heidegger was only seriously committed to German nationalism (in the romantic sense by which it was expressed by the Nazis), but not anti-Semitism or the holocaust. Heidegger was not a Nazi in a sense that is does not admit of the deep repugnance we attach to the label. Rockmore's search for evidence of Nazism in Heidegger's philosophy is ironic because he warns that we must define what Nazism means for Heidegger.

Psychologically, Heidegger's attraction to Nazism was rooted in opportunism (to promote himself), egoism (the desire to be the spiritual

---

13. Rockmore, *On Heidegger's*, 54, 75.
14. Ibid., 284.

father of a political movement) and personal disposition (to reproduce the folk-truths, and memories, he grew up with).

On January 20, 1948, writing to Herbert Marcuse, he compared the "Jews" to the "East Germans," failing to grasp the meaning of the "holocaust."[15] Contemptible as Heidegger's Nazism is, more so is the fact he never had a change of heart. It is as if, blinded by German nationalism, a core aspect of his identity, self-assured as having a place as a great philosopher, he was unwilling to take in what Nazism in fact meant.

Philosophically, what are more worrisome than Heidegger's political boondoggles are the contradictions that plague his work if he is to be a Nazi. First, in his infamous speech "The Self-Determination of the German University," Heidegger identified German greatness with science. He seems at once a romantic critic of the effects of technology, and at the same time a spokesperson for German science.

We are left perplexed to whether Heidegger is against the scientism, or supports its advancement, provided it is of the German variety. His famous *Der Spiegl* interview was titled "Only a God Can Save Us Now."[16] Heidegger thinks that the beginning of science is good, though lost to us, and its authentic fruition¾with being¾is yet to come. His statements for and against science remain confounding.

Yet Heidegger's philosophy provided the basis for a critique of technology and Nazism. Heidegger wrote, "Agriculture is now a mechanized food industry in essence the same as the manufacturing of corpses in gas chambers and extermination camps, same as blockade and starvation of nations, the same as the production of hydrogen bombs."[17]

Heidegger's comparison between modern agriculture and the gas chambers is often seen as evidence of his insensitivity to the holocaust.[18] Yet, as Safranski points out, Heidegger's remarks on agriculture need not be offensive.[19] Heidegger's critique of technology was a criticism of viewing things solely as means to ends. Be it the destruction of rain forests, marine ecology, or the prevalence of factory farms with their attendant disassembly plants, the mechanization of life and death is captured in Heidegger's

---

15. Farías, *Heidegger and Nazism*, 285.

16. *Der Spiegl's* interview with M. Heidegger, trans., M. Alter and J. D. Caputo in *Philosophy Today* 20, April 4, 1976, 267–85.

17. As cited in Farías, *Heidegger and Nazism*, 287; Rockmore, *On Heidegger's*, 241.

18. Farías, *Heidegger and Nazism*, xi.

19. Safranski, *Martin Heidegger*, 414.

critique. From an environmental point of view, his critique of technology is prophetic.

Second, Safranski points out that Heidegger's support for the Nazi war against the Allies seems at odds with what he said in his Nietzsche Lectures.[20] In the Nietzsche Lectures, Heidegger said war is the will-to-power and the oblivion of being. He seeks out a relationship with being (*Bezug zon Seyn*), and supporting what would, for him, make that impossible¾war.[21]

Heidegger's misadventures in politics, however, also illustrate the romantic thrust of his works. It is desirable to separate Heidegger's philosophy from his politics. Expunging his nationalist sentiments does no harm to Heidegger's original reading of figures in the history of Western philosophy, critique of technology, or overall view.

THE CHARGE OF OBSCURITY

Paul Edwards, in *Heidegger's Confusions*, has attempted to scrutinize the sense of some of the claims Heidegger makes. Edwards made some observations that Heideggerians need to take seriously. Unfortunately, however, his account is marred with polemics. Edwards, following unwittingly in the tradition of Descartes, indicated his pre-determined conclusion in his preface, "Bertrand Russell once referred to Kant as the greatest catastrophe in the history of philosophy. C. D. Broad commented that this position surely belonged to Hegel. Both Russell and Broad were wrong, because this title undoubtedly belongs to Martin Heidegger."[22]

Edward's position is partly slanted, both in terms of tone and personal attacks. Edwards described books on Heidegger as being of a "devotional nature."[23] There is some truth to the contention that Heidegger had attracted a devout following. Yet, he also calls Stambaugh, a translator of *Being and Time*, "a leading American Sheppardess."[24] A Heidegger scholar, if male, may be referred to as a "Sheppard."[25] His tone hangs heavy with sarcasm.

20. Ibid., 328–29.
21. Ibid., 286.
22. Edwards, *Heidegger's Confusions*, 9.
23. Ibid., 11.
24. Ibid., 30.
25. Ibid., 42.

Romanticism Revisited

Edwards has to explain why, however, if Heidegger is such a worthless philosopher ("the greatest catastrophe," as Edwards put it), he has such prominence. Edwards explains: "Heidegger will continue to fascinate those hungry for mysticism of the anaemic and purely verbal variety... The odds are that people afflicted in this way will exist for a long time; and if this is so, Heidegger will indeed be read and admired for centuries. More sober and rational persons will continue to regard the whole Heidegger phenomenon as a grotesque aberration of the human mind."[26] Edwards is an example, by his own standard, of a candidate for being of a sober and rational mind.

Edwards does point to difficulties in making sense of some of what Heidegger said. For instance, he points out that, for Heidegger, ontological difference entails that being cannot be the same as nature.[27] The claim that Heidegger is engaged in sophistry gains steam when we find it difficult to make sense of the being-question.

Edwards also scrutinized Heidegger's claim that we always die alone.[28] He points out that we could die with someone, for instance, if we committed suicide with our friends. He finds Heidegger's claim either trivially true or false.[29] Edwards claims that what Heidegger said is "non-sense," or at odds with a "grammatical truth."[30]

He concludes, in a particularly damming statement for this project, "The emptiness of the Heideggerian doctrine, what may not unfairly be described as its bogus character, becomes particularly clear when one reflects that it *seems* to, but does not in fact, have any practical implications."[31] In his acknowledgements, he finds it relevant to point out that, furthermore, "German is my native language and I had little difficulty translating Heidegger himself even when this meant translating meaningless German into meaningless English."[32]

Yet, Heidegger's claims about death, which Edwards finds meaningless, or false, for example, is plainly understood by anyone not subjected to years of formal education in philosophy. In a Heideggerian sense, we do not die alone, for example, to extent that the world we occupy shapes how

26. Ibid.
27. Ibid., 46.
28. Ibid., 50.
29. Ibid., 64.
30. Ibid., 57, 61.
31. Ibid., 56.
32. Ibid., 123.

we view death. Nevertheless, physical death is, it is reasonable to claim, a very private affair. For instance, in an experience I had speaking to a cancer patient, I was struck of how her description of what it was like to approach death entailed the falling away of value, for friends, family, property; she just wanted to live. Even Heidegger, at any rate, noted, in his later years, that approaching physical death is much different than theorizing about it.[33]

It is indeed striking that in disciplines such as biology, physics, and mathematics, where there is actually knowledge to be had, there are disagreements, but rarely is the tone as virulent as that that we encounter in Edwards critique, or philosophy generally. Benecerraf, the Princeton philosopher of mathematics, had pointed out that philosophy is the discipline where it is commonplace to think others views preposterous, but less common is to recognize our own as so.[34]

Heidegger provided interesting readings of some of the major figures in the history of western philosophy (his reading of Kant) and, by his very use of language, opened up new avenues for academic philosophy. For others, he was, as Dummett put it years earlier, a "a figure of fun."[35] Most likely, both pro- and anti-Heideggerians, have a valid point, from their perspectives. Assessments of Heidegger often reflect our interests and the style in which we think philosophy should be done.

Heidegger cannot be written off as the ramblings of someone who is not using language correctly. Edwards' view, at moments, is as silly as finding fault with James Joyce's *Ulysses*, for grammatical transgressions.

Sure, the theme of quackery dogs Heidegger. As I have suggested, his questions (e.g., what is the meaning of being?) are obscure. He sometimes seems to wish to dismiss contradictions in his thought by saying he is "on the way." Edwards may be right in his psychological profile of the Heideggerian (that seeks out mysticism), but that does not speak to the truth, or intelligibility, of the claims. In a discipline self-conscious about its legitimacy, there is desire, with a parallel in the sciences, to isolate quacks. Yet, mysticism is not quackery; it is just a view about the relationship between the mind and world.

It is important to notice that Edwards employs the jargon of ordinary language philosophers, who attempted to discover that philosophical problems were just mistakes in how we use symbolic systems. The positivists

---

33. Ott, *Martin Heidegger*, 369.
34. Benecerraf, "What Mathematical Truth."
35. Dummett, *Truth and Other Enigmas*.

attempted to deem what is meaningful or not. Yet philosophers have likely never discovered anything about language, any more than previous metaphysicians had discovered the stuff of the universe.

POET AND OBSCUREST

Heidegger's poet of a destitute time, Hölderlin, shall now be considered further. As in real estate, so too is the case with philosophy. Location is everything, so we begin with the setting. Heidegger hails from Messkrich, a small German town between Lake Constance, the Swabian Alp Mountains and the Upper Danube.[36]

Hölderlin transforms into art the visions of the place from which Heidegger may recollect:

> Waft coolness to warm shores from the open sea / While under potent sun beams the grape matures, / And, oh, where still golden autumn / Turns into songs the poor people's sighing.[37]

We read of being driven from what is familiar, both as a man that must leave his youth, a people its land, and a culture its time. Hölderlin wrote:

> Besides, when I was younger / Someone confided to me / That time out of mind our parents / The German people, had quietly / Departed from the waves of the Danube . . . / And none could comprehend / The other's peculiar speech, a quarrel.[38]

The estrangement ends in the loss of the ancestral language. Hölderlin wrote, "Begging for rest; so a wounded deer will flee the forests."[39] Hölderlin, in "To the Virgin Mary," wrote, "To the inaccessible / Primordial vault / of the forest, / the Occident."[40] We read, in "The Journey": "Most happy Swabia, my mother . . . / Innate in you is loyalty. For whatever dwells / Close to its origin is loathe to leave the place."[41]

The romanticism also speaks to what is to come. For Hölderlin, there is a glimpse of renewal:

36. Safranski, *Martin Heidegger*, 3.
37. Hamburger, *Freiedrich Hölderlin*, 23.
38. Ibid., 395.
39. Ibid., 233.
40. Ibid., 393.
41. Ibid.

Part I: Everyday Ethics

> Stay with us two until on communal ground, reunited / Where, when their coming is due, all the blessed souls will return . . .[42]

The Christian allusions are inescapable. The final guiding principle of the self, where we are to go is given reassurance.

In his lectures of 1942 Heidegger analyized *Der Ister* (i.e., the Danube), which beckons us to where he was from. Rudolf Stadelmann was a professor of modern history and acting Dean of the Faculty of Philosophy at the University of Tübingen; he was also a longtime admirer of Heidegger. On September 23, 1946, dismissed from his teaching post Heidegger wrote to Stadelmann. Instead of criticizing the grounds of his dismissal, he found it relevant to write: "I have the feeling that another hundred years of neglect are needed before people start to realize what Hölderlin's poetry holds in store."[43] He ends by citing Hölderlin, with, in the context of dismissal, the following cryptic lines:

> Long is
> The time, but the Truth
> Is fulfilled

Alluded to by Hölderlin, it is the Black Forest, so dear to Germans, that resonated with Heidegger.

To be sure, Heidegger must have taken pleasure when awarded the Hebel Prize by his native town of Messkrich, the *Land* of Baden—Württenbuerg.[44] Demonstrating his unrepentant romanticism, Heidegger in some later writings, adopts an older spelling of "*Sein*," by substituting a "y," "*Seyn*."

Rainer Maria Rilke, also captured the inevitability of history that reminds us of Heidegger story of being, "Even if we don't will it, / God matures."[45] There are stages:

> He like a ring / the homeless encloses. / He passes in mantles and metamorphoses / through the ascending voices of Time.[46]

---

42. Ibid., 241.
43. Ott, *Martin Heidegger*, 19.
44. Ibid., 366.
45. Rilke, *Selected Works*, 34.
46. Ibid., 41.

Allusions to divinity, in Rilke's writings, are set amidst loss, "Men are but chances, voices, brokenness."[47] Fate mingles with tragedy. As Rilke wrote:

> How do the houses appear / to them, those graves, and for the all too small figures of lovers, apart,— / oh, the leaves, lifted by winds of longing / in the books of the lonely?[48]

However much Heidegger wished to distance himself from Christianity, and Catholicism specifically, his philosophy is configured in a manner that is not that different from the narrative of the reckoning Rilke wrote of. Rilke's inevitability and sense of tragedy is reflected in Heidegger's story of being.

The literature of isolation, disenfranchisement, and meaningless was an impressive expression of an aspect of the state of culture of the modern world. The holocaust literature adds chilling detail.

Insofar as poets are intended to be prophetic, we turn to O. E. Mandelstam, who was born in Warrsaw, in 1891, the son of a Jewish leather merchant. He articulated both the dream and the tragedy that are the lot of romantics. First the dream:

> To read as children read, / to think as children think, / to blow away everything large, / to rise up out of sorrow. / I'm tired to death of life, / I don't want any, / but I love my miserable country / having known none other. / In a garden, far away, I swung / on a wooden swing, / and I still remember the dark, tall trees / though a feverish mist.[49]

The darker side of human history finds expression in The *Voronezh Notebooks*, specifically his "Poem to an Unknown Solider." Mandelstam wrote of: The incorruptible sky over the trenches, / a sky of vast wholesale deaths . . . / Aortas are flooded with blood / as a whisper runs though the ranks."[50] Mandelstam transforms what is otherwise pleasant into its inverse, "There are women, who are so close to the moist earth; there every step is a loud mourning . . . / flowers are immortal. Heaven is integral. / What will be is only a promise."[51]

47. Ibid., 69.
48. Ibid., 336.
49. Mandelstam, *Voronezh Notebooks*, 32.
50. Ibid., 84–85.
51. Ibid., 95.

Mandelstam captured the darker side of Heidegger's writings, paralleling what he said about technology. The Black Forest has been felled, the Danube is not fit for drinking out of, and all around are corpses. Tragedy flows through the writings of Hölderlin, Rilke, and Mandelstam, so too, Heidegger.

THE FALL OF ROME

We witness these poetic sentiments detailed as history in Spengler's *Decline of the West*, published in 1918. Heidegger lectured on Spengler as early as 1920.[52]

In the early pages of *Decline of the West*, Spengler wrote: "In this book is attempted for the first time the venture of predetermining history, of following the still untravelled stages in the destiny of Culture, and specifically of the only Culture of our time and on our planet which is actually in the phase of fulfilment—the West-European—America."[53]

Spengler is interested in what he calls the "metaphysical structure" of history.[54] He claims the West is unique in having a history (i.e., a written record of what has gone before).[55]

He wrote, "Before us there stands a last spiritual crisis that will involve all of Europe and America . . . Exact science must fall upon its own keen sword."[56] Destiny, for the Germans, looms large. Spengler explains, "For me, 'people' is a *unity of the soul*. The great events of history were not really achieved by people; they themselves created people."[57] For the German idealists, being was identified with history (as opposed to, for example, nature); we were thought of pawns pushed on by events—ideas—greater than ourselves. Spengler wrote: "Only with the end of grand History does holy, still Being reappear. It is a drama noble in its aimlessness as the stars, the rotation of the earth, and the alternation of the land and sea, of ice and the virgin forest upon its face. We may marvel at it or lament it—but it is there."[58]

52. Ott, *Martin Heidegger*, 219.
53. Spengler, *Decline of the West*, 1:3.
54. Ibid., 3.
55. Ibid., 15.
56. Ibid., 424.
57. Spengler, *Decline of the West*, 2:165.
58. Ibid., 435.

Spengler is committed to the notion of destiny, as is indicated by some of the final words in his work: "And a task that historic necessity has set *will* be accomplished with the individual or against him."[59] We could wonder if Spengler did indeed identify being with history. Yet Spengler's poetic utterances need not be submitted to philosophical scrutiny to capture the connection to Heidegger.

Heidegger, like Spengler, aggrandized history, metaphysically. According to Heidegger philosophers articulate the ideas of their milieu. For Heidegger, also, there is the contention that we are in a state of decline. Heidegger claimed that Aristotle's *Physics* was to determine two millennium of Western thought. The orientation of scientific inquiry was laid in the *Physics*, where we analyze problems into parts. Let us now turn to the psychological perspective of Maslow for what a being relationship could be like.

THE PSYCHOLOGY OF THE BEING-RELATIONSHIP

Maslow's psychology is juxtaposed to various schools, which are often consider prey to scientism (e.g., behavioral, reductionism etc.), with the premise that the individual "is an integrated, organized whole."[60] Maslow concentrated on the "total personality" and how we attempt to solve "life problems."[61]

Neurosis, he tells us, is a breakdown in behavior, occurring in situations of stress. Maslow provided the example of a sheep that is required to do a task. Yet when the task becomes so difficult that it cannot be done, the sheep will become neurotic.[62] Maslow wrote, "[G]ood life circumstances are among the *ultimate* therapeutic agents."[63] The goal of the psychotherapeutic situation is to increase self-esteem and security (replacing helplessness, worthlessness, guilt, and fear of catastrophic breakdown, emphasizing strengths).[64] As Maslow said, "The only satisfactory way of understanding

---

59. Ibid., 507.

60. Maslow, *Motivation and Personality*, 3; Maslow and Mittelmann, *Principles of Abnormal Psychology*, ix, 109.

61. Maslow and Mittelmann, *Principles of Abnormal Psychology*, 8, 14.

62. Ibid., 23–25.

63. Maslow, *Towards a Psychology of Being*, 93, 96.

64. Maslow and Mittelmann, *Principles of Abnormal Psychology*, 179, 181; Maslow, *Motivation and Personality*, 6, 9, 22, 76.

how a geopolitical environment becomes a psychological environment is to understand that the principle of the psychological environment is the current goal of the organism in that particular environment."[65]

Maslow wrote, "It is quite true that humans live by bread alone—when there is no bread."[66] That is to say, safety needs must be first satisfied (see Table 1, "Maslow's Hierarchy of Needs").[67]

Table 1.
Maslow's Hierarchy of Needs

Type of Need	Specific Need
B. Higher-Order Needs (Being-cognition)	9. Self-actualization
	8. Aesthetic appreciation
	7. Understanding
	6. Knowing
A. Lower-Order Needs (Deficiency-cognition)	5. Esteem
	4. Love
	3. Belongingness
	2. Safety
	1. Survival

As Maslow put it, "What humans *can* be, they *must* be."[68] According to him, the psychology of Being and becoming are reconciled by fulfilling both lower and higher needs.[69] Basic needs, he noted, are more elaborate than behaviorists contend because they represent "a theory of the ends and

---

65. Maslow, *Motivation and Personality*, 11.
66. Ibid., 17.
67. Ibid., 19, 26.
68. Ibid., 22.
69. Maslow, *Towards a Psychology of Being*, 56.

ROMANTICISM REVISITED

ultimate values of the organism."⁷⁰ Higher needs are the result of later evolutionary development, he said.⁷¹

Lower-order needs must be met to feel fruition of larger "personal, social, intellectual issues."⁷² He pointed out, however, once we have experienced higher-order gratification, we are likely to forgo lower-order ones for them, though both exist in a "synergic" relationship.⁷³

Maslow commented on the ethical implications of his project, "The philosopher of ethics has much to learn from a close examination of human motivational life. If our noblest impulses are not seen as check reins, on horses, and if our animal needs are seen to be of the same nature as our highest needs, how can a sharp dichotomy are maintained?"⁷⁴

Self-actualization may be facilitated, according to Maslow, by what he called "peak experiences."⁷⁵ He distinguished Being-cognition (B-cognition), that is, apprehending being, from deficiency-needs-cognition (D-cognition), that is, apprehending our needs. B-cognition is characterized by Maslow as being more passive and receptive than D-cognition.⁷⁶ Maslow did not think B-cognition as apathy, however. He remarked, "They [critics] interpret 'let-be' as neglect, or lack of love, or even contempt."⁷⁷ He explained, "My thesis is then: we can in principle, have a descriptive naturalistic science of human values; that the age-old mutually exclusive contrast between 'what is' and 'who I ought to be' is in part a false one; that we can study the highest values or goals of human beings as we study the values of ants or horses or oak trees, for that matter, Martians."⁷⁸

As with many psychologists, Maslow's thought arose from his own needs: "I was isolated and unhappy. I grew up in libraries and among books, without friends."⁷⁹ Maslow's thought illuminates Heidegger's in these respects. First, Maslow emphasized the meaning of experiences to the individual, which reflects the Heideggerian notion that Dasien ex-

---

70. Maslow, *Motivation and Personality*, 35.
71. Ibid., 37, 41, 53, 57.
72. Ibid., 41.
73. Ibid., 14, 57.
74. Ibid., 60.
75. Maslow, *Towards a Psychology of Being*, 76–77.
76. Ibid., 81.
77. Ibid., 113.
78. Ibid., 157.
79. Maslow, *Personality and Motivation*, xxxvi.

ists in-the-world (-in-decline). Maslow allows us to extend some of the implications of being-in-the-world, focusing on when conflicts arise within any one.

Second, looking to the "total person" in a process of attempting to obtain goals, Maslow offers an alternative embodied account of values. Maslow thinks that ethics can be based on a scientific understanding of human nature, which may reasonably think at least parallel Heidegger's fundamental ontology.

Third, Heidegger's entire critique of technology, and hence bureaucratization, is also written into his search for being and authentic relations. The modern world increases, for Maslow, our propensity towards mental illness because it frustrates our desire to obtain our basic needs of belonging. Finally, both see a need for a mystical experience ("peak experience") to obtain self-actualization—B-cognition, as Maslow dubbed it.

Heidegger gave a philosophical voice to the intellectual ethos of post-World War II Europe, which was disgusted with the efficient application of technologically for killing other human beings. Yet admittedly, Heidegger's figurative use of language, undoubtedly, has made it difficult to separate the tragedies of Sophocles, the poems of Hölderlin, novels of Steinbeck, or the historical narratives of Spangler, from philosophy.

The blurring of various forms of literature is important when we consider ethics, however. Ethics has traditionally been transmitted through stories, passed along at the bedside, campfire, or recorded for the decipherment of an elite class. Ethics, before it was submitted to philosophical reflection, was a practice of enacted stories (discussion in chapter 9). In fact, Maslow offers a psychological perspective that potentially explains how ethics springs from the meeting of needs that runs the gambit from belonging to the apprehension of being.

Yet as we have seen, the continuing ambiguity of Heidegger's writings is demonstrated by scholars' often resolute interpretations of his works as simultaneously anti-metaphysical, though retaining a mystical element.[80] In part II, I shall consider how Heidegger's thought can reasonably be said to terminate in mysticism.

---

80. Sikka, *Forms of Transcendence*.

PART II

Interlude: Being and Ethics

5

Ethics and Time

Heidegger asks, "Is there a way which leads from primordial time to the meaning of Being?"[1] For Heidegger, the being-relationship was to be the basis of his ethics, yet that was suggested needs to be transformed into a question about primordial time. If we are not to just pass the buck, replacing the mystery of being with the mystery of time, we must look deeply into what he has to say about it. Further, at least since Plato, our metaphysical commitments have entailed ethical consequences.

Heidegger's early writings, like *The Concept of Time*, *Being and Time*, and *The Basic Problems of Phenomenology* are where we first encounter the tension between the question he posed—what is the meaning of *being*?—and his ability to say anything about it. Notoriously, in *Being and Time*, he evaded the question, and engaged in an analysis of Dasein. In this chapter, I shall use his discussion of time as an analogy for the problem he faced with the being-question as it relates to ethics. I shall leave aside his later writings, considering them in chapter 6.

I proceed in the following way. First, I consider Heidegger's attempt to dismantle the problem of time by a recovery of primordial time (some pretheoretical concept of time). Second, I claim, it remains a veritable mystery, at least up to 1927, how Heidegger could go on to say anything about what time is, and from what little he does say, I try to draw out consequences for his ethics.

1. *BT*, 488.

Part II: Interlude: Being and Ethics

RETROSPECTIVE TO THE LOSS OF PRIMORDIAL TIME

For Plato, we have two worlds: an eternal, unchanging realm, which gives birth to a temporal one where change occurs.[2] Time as an image of eternity, gives rise to knowledge that is subjective (*doxa*) not objective (*sophia*). Depending upon our ontological commitments, however, time may be viewed as either unreal (Plato's shadows) or real (Plotinus' mysticism).

According to Heidegger, for Aristotle, time was linked to, or said to accompany, motion and change.[3] As Heidegger said, "Aristotle does not pursue this question any further; he merely touches on it, which leads to the question how time itself exists."[4] Since time accompanies motion, are we to think of it like a "container," in which case it is real?[5] Heidegger notes, within the ordinary conception of time, the idea of its subjectivity or objectivity can arise.[6] Or, are we to think of time as something we impose upon the world by counting, in which case it would seem to be ideal? Heidegger noted that Aristotle does not answer the question.[7]

Augustine famously said, "If no one asks me, I know: if I wish to explain it to one that asketh, I know not [what time is]."[8] For Heidegger, the very idea of a "now," which Augustine took to be real, is the most abstract notion of time contingent upon the advent of the clock.[9] The clock allows a positing of identical, temporal points that can be fixed.[10] Where the "now" may mean numerous things, this year, for example, the clock brings to the fore the abstract idea of "now."[11]

With the ordinary conception of time as an endless sequence of time-slices, we assume that each now has some precise measurement.[12] Yet according to Heidegger, time has no length.[13] The present never really implies

---

2. *T*, 37D.
3. Aristotle, *Physics* 218b30, 223a20.
4. *BP*, 254.
5. Ibid., 238.
6. *BT*, 374, 471, 457.
7. *BP*, 254.
8. Augustine, *Confessions* §11.14
9. Ibid., §11.17–8.
10. *CT*, 4.
11. *BT*, 474.
12. *BP*, 269.
13. *CT*, 15.

exactness, primordially.[14] We could say, Augustine is allowed to puzzle over the ontology of time because he is dealing with what Heidegger calls ordinary time. Also, from Heidegger's standpoint, ordinary time becomes internalized and constitutive of experience in Husserl's thought.

Husserl's treatment of time, although a phenomenologist who set about to avoid both idealism and realism, seems to internalize this clock time.[15] Husserl appeals to notions such as present sensations, past memories (retention), and fantasies of the future (protention).[16] Husserl tried to explain why we think experience occurs in the present (present-ation).[17]

Going back to the everyday, for Heidegger, ordinary time is constituted by the past, present, and future, a succession of nows.[18] Heidegger wrote: "What then is time and how does it exist? Is it only subjective, or is it only objective, or is it neither the one nor the other?"[19]

Heidegger not only elucidated Aristotle's discussion of time, but is the editor of Husserl's famous treatment of time.[20] Heidegger proposed to go back to "primordial time" by way of an analysis of "ordinary time."[21] He considers how it is that we encounter time in the world, as a way to laying bare its ground.[22]

Heidegger pointed out that time is first encountered when we deal with things.[23] For example, when Dasein sets out do deal with any one piece of equipment; it does so in terms of time. Dasein has to reckon with time, and even measures it to this end.[24] For example, we think "now I have to make lunch," or "now that my book is missing."[25] I check a clock to see "how much time I have to do this or that."[26] When we think about things, we do

---

14. *BP,* 266, 268–70.
15. *H,* 23, 66. Dostal, "Time and Phenomonology," 148.
16. *H,* 142.
17. Ibid., 152, 160.
18. *BP,* 261; *BT,* 374–75.
19. Ibid., 255.
20. *H,* 15–16.
21. *BT,* 474.
22. *CT,* 7.
23. *BT,* 457.
24. *CT,* 15.
25. *BT,* 461.
26. *BP,* 258.

so in terms of time: "How much longer till I have to lecture?," "when is class over," and so on.[27]

Insofar as time is not first encountered as an abstract philosophical question—is it real?—but in our concernful dealings with things, time, Heidegger claims, is either right or wrong: "Look, this is the wrong time . . . etc."[28] If autumn is coming and we start to sow wheat, it is "the wrong time."[29]

Time, he notes, is datable, spanned and public.[30] Heidegger wrote: "The dating can be calendrically indeterminate but it is nevertheless determined by a particular historical happening or some other event . . . The 'now when,' 'at-the-time when,' and 'then when' are related essentially to an entity that gives a date to the dateable . . . by its very structure, always already related to something, and in its expression is more or less definitely dated from something."[31] We may date things according to the rising and setting of the sun, the birth of a prophet, and so on. Time has a significance because we measure it, by some calendar or astronomy, in order to use it.[32] The significance embodies a totality of relationships, which are by no means private. As Heidegger said, "The now is not the sort of thing that only one or another of us could find out; it is not something about which one of us might perhaps know but another might not; rather, in the Dasein's being-with-one-another itself, in their communal being-in-the-world, there is already present the unity of temporality itself open for itself."[33] Time is a public phenomenon insofar as Dasein, per se, is Being-in-a-world.

Even though ordinary time of modern persons, Heidegger said, is clock-time; any dating system, he notes, has the characteristic of "measuring," which serves as a "standard."[34] It is the standardization provided by a shared measure of time that allows its public character.[35] Heidegger wrote: "The measurement of time gives it a marked public character, so that only in this way does what we generally call 'the time' become well

---

27. *BT*, 464.
28. *BP*, 262, 271.
29. *BT*, 467; *BP*, 258–59.
30. *BT*, 467; *BP*, 273.
31. *BP*, 263.
32. *BT*, 423.
33. *BP*, 270.
34. *BT*, 469–67.
35. *BP*, 264.

known."³⁶ "We" for example may all recognize night and day, spring and fall, the end of the semester, and so on, depending upon the world we dwell in. If I said it was, for example "2:30 p.m.," you could only understand this by virtue of understanding the same measure being employed: the clock. Heidegger said, "The clock that one has, every clock, shows the time of being-with-one-another-in-the-world."³⁷

From primordial time, we arrive at ordinary time as a succession of nows, and further, conceive these moments to go on forever.³⁸ As Wood, a commentator on the philosophy of time, points out, the structure of all involvements are temporal and expose a towards which.³⁹ In fact, the clock, as with other dating systems, shows how "we measure time because we need to use time."⁴⁰

The "we," who is using time, is the universal Dasein. In order to go to the roots of time, as it were, Heidegger explored how time is possible for the being that is-there. Heidegger has tried to recover a primordial, finite time which is instrumentally efficacious. Not only does the infinite remain unclear, but it covers up, said Heidegger, primordial time. We could say, for Heidegger, ordinary time conceals primordial time, which is grounded in Dasein's state of fallenness.⁴¹

DASEIN AS TIME

Dasein, said Heidegger, is not in time, but "is time itself."⁴² Time is not something real in which we are located, as if it were some sort of big container; rather: "Time is Dasein."⁴³ The way we first deal with time, for Heidegger, is in terms of the future: in-order-to, for-the-sake-of. We use things, like a hammer, in order to achieve things in the future: to hang the picture on the wall. Thus, ordinary time, as an irreversible succession of indivisible

---

36. *BT*, 471.
37. *CT*, 17.
38. *BT*, 379, 474, 476; *BP*, 259, 272.
39. Wood, *Deconstruction of Time*, 230.
40. *BP*, 260.
41. *BT*, 379; *BP*, 271.
42. *CT*, 14.
43. *CT*, 20; *BP*, 255; *BT*, 375, 377, 401.

points, could be called vacuous insofar as it suggests a separation from "how" we use time.[44]

For Heidegger, time is not a "such and such . . . a what" but a "how." Time is not a thing, but a means to an end. Hence, Heidegger wrote, the "most appropriate manner of access to and of dealing with time as in each case mine."[45] As Heidegger has argued, we reckon with it. Time is part of our world. Time is ready-at-hand in-order-to.

Heidegger attempts to avoid the problem of time as subjective or objective by what Dostal calls a transcendental argument.[46] This argument uncovers the conditions that allow for the possibility of time in the first place. Namely, primordial time is presupposed for any conception of time. Moreover, the ground of primordial time, Dasein, becomes the ultimate ground of all conceptions of time. Yet, we cannot ask which the correct conception of time is. All we can say is that we have different conceptions of time—perhaps in different epochs—that arise from different dating systems rooted in different worlds.

Even though primordial time is the ground of all other conceptions, we cannot even say "that is what time is." Rather, we can only say, "that is how we think about time." Yet, as Wood remarks, in a similar vein, "One might still wonder whether this 'public time' was something we imagine, project, impose upon the real world, or whether it was really there."[47] It remains questionable whether the recovery of primordial time overcomes the problem of time's subjectivity or objectivity.

In fact, are we not forced to reconcile ourselves to the fact that any one conception of time is just, using the term of a philosopher of science, J. J. Earman, a "convention"?[48] Primordial time seems to collapse into idealism. As Wood also notes, it may be suggested that temporality is being considered in a very much subjectivist perspective, in terms of Dasein.[49]

At best, we could say that the problem of time's subjectivity or objectivity arises from dealing with a certain conception of it that is far removed

---

44. *CT*, 21.

45. *CT*, 22; *BP*, 270. What Heidegger calls "ordinary time" in *Basic Problems of Phenomenology*, I call "primordial time" in order to remain consistent to when "ordinary time" refers to how encounter time, before Heidegger's analysis.

46. Dostal, "Time and Phenomenology," 150–53.

47. Wood, *Deconstruction of Time*, 239.

48. Earman, "Till the End of Time," 132.

49. Wood, *Deconstruction of Time*, 230.

ETHICS AND TIME

from its ground in the primordial sense. However, there seems to remain a difference between (1) to know a particular way in which time is conceived and (2) to make a claim about what time is. Since we can never adjudicate between the different conceptions of time as being correct, it does not seem that Heidegger avoids the problem of time: We can always ask, "which conception is really time?" He wrote: "'Time' is present-at-hand neither in the 'subject' not in the 'Object,' neither 'inside' nor 'outside'; the condition for the very possibility of this 'earlier.'"[50]

It is not that the issue of time's subjectivity or objectivity does not arise or that we could not understand what is meant by the question. Indeed, Heidegger has shown such a question could come about. The question is meaningless in this sense: It ask a question that cannot be answered. The reason the question admits of no answer is because the question is confused. Time is not objective or subjective, but objective if and only if subjective: "Both answers—time is objective and time is subjective—get their own right in a certain way from the original conception of temporality."[51]

There is another reason to view Heidegger's argument as overcoming the problem of time as subjective or objective. Here, we have to emphasize time's relation to "worldhood." Heidegger maintains, "Dasein is its world existingly."[52] As Wood also points out, time "belongs to"[53] the world.

We can consider Heidegger's formulation "Being-in-the-world," which has a rather expansive significance. Briefly, it is supposed to indicate that Dasein (as subject) is not apart from a world (as object), but is subject-object, so to speak, even though the terminology is unHeideggerian. Similarly, time is no more subjective than objective: it is part of our world. For Heidegger, Dasein and the world are an equiprimoridal co-happening. And, insofar as time is part of my world, it belongs to me; it is neither internal or external.

By delimiting how it is possible to think about time, Heidegger would have avoided the problem of time as ideal or real. Here, how we think about time is indistinguishable from what time is. A consequence arises, however: It does not seem possible to make any ontological claims about time if we are merely left with several different conceptions, which we cannot think outside of. We would, so it seems, always be left with knowing how we think

50. *BT*, 472.
51. *BP*, 256.
52. *BT*, 416, 476.
53. Wood, *Deconstruction of Time*, 240.

about time, but never with knowing what it is. In fact, for Heidegger, we can never know what time is in-itself precisely because we cannot comprehend time outside of how we think about it. We cannot think about time as if it were separate from our Being-the-world. In Heidegger's terms, I know how to use time according to the measure of a certain dating system, but not how to explain what it really is, since such questions are not answerable.

The upshot of Heidegger's account of time for his prospective ethics goes like this. Primordial ethics will be rooted in a world of practices. To asks blankly about if so-and-so is right or wrong is to problematize ethics, in a similar way we had done with both time and being: what is real and what not, what is true or false, and in the context of ethics, what is right or wrong. Adopting Heidegger's phraseology, we can say that we should avoid an ordinary ethics in favor for something more fundamental. So far I have argued that we know that a primary ethics will arise from a way of being where we are in the correct relationship with being, hence, living a life of letting beings be. Surely, we will have to add more detail to this picture to make it plausible, but for the time being we can console ourselves by having composed a sense of direction in which we are headed.

We admittedly have a better idea of what sort of questions not to ask, than how to answer the one Heidegger puts before us, namely, about the meaning of being. Yet given his insistence that ethics must be founded on the being-relationship, we are prompted to confront the nature of that in greater detail.

6

Ontological Similarity

The claim is that Aristotle set out to consider being but ended up only dealing with beings.[1] The charge has often been laid against Aristotle that he never had ontology.[2] Heidegger's grievance, with many figures within the Western tradition, lies in their forgetfulness of being.[3] In this chapter I shall explain how answering the being-question requires mysticism. The difference of being from beings Heidegger calls ontological difference, and is presupposed for asking whether ontology, in Aristotle's sense, is even possible.

I proceed by first laying out the problem ontological difference poses for ontology. Second, I briefly consider Heidegger's explanation of ontological difference as ground in Dasein. Third, I argue that, for him, there is a similitude between being and beings. I argue that mysticism allows us to make sense of Heidegger's pursuit.

THE PROBLEM

Heidegger noted that Aristotle distinguished between four causes: the material, formal, efficient, and final.[4] Basically, it was hoped that by an identification of each cause, we could provide an exhaustive explanation of

---

1. Aristotle, *Metaphysics* 1003a25, 1042a29, 1017b25; Aristotle, *Categories* 1a.
2. Owens, *Doctrine of Being*, 36.
3. Knasas, "Heideggerian Critique," 415.
4. Aristotle, *Metaphysics* 1013a25. Also see *ER*, 5.

what any one thing essentially is. Whereas Aristotle thought he was doing ontology by explaining what any one thing essentially is— especially in relation to the final cause—Heidegger has several criticisms.

First, Aristotle is not considering being (ontology), but beings (the ontic realm). Aristotle, by way of the causes, can tell us about this or that being, but not being as such. Second, according to Heidegger, Aristotle passed over the transcendental ground of his causes. Whereas the causes are supposed to answer the most fundamental question—the *why* of any one thing—they themselves have a reason. As Heidegger says, "The primordiality of transcendental grounds and their peculiar character as grounds remain hidden in Aristotle's formal characterization of the 'first' and 'highest' beginnings."[5]

Gilson, the renowned medievalist, remarks that just as numbers can be said to share in a characteristic of quantity, the world is sometimes claimed to be one.[6] The idea is that there is something common to all things in the world just as a unit of quantity could be said to be common to all numbers.

The idea, however, of being, as that which is most general, quickly poses a problem. One can abstract *humanity* from Socrates or *life* from a living being. What happens if we are not speaking of (1) a lion, (2) a cat, (3) an animal, (4) a living thing, (5) a thing, but just (6) being? The point is that each category can contain the one before it so that, for instance, *animal* includes *lion* and *cat*. But being is abstract. Indeed, the problem is not just that the idea of being is difficult to conceptualize, but whether it even makes sense. Heidegger, for instance, points out that one cannot buy "fruit" but always has to buy apples, oranges, grapes, and so on. As he say, "It is infinitely more impossible to represent 'Being' as the general characteristics of particular beings."[7]

In fact, according to Owen, an Aristotle scholar, it is because of extreme abstraction that Kant deemed being as vacuous, empty and indeterminate.[8] Kant, following the Wolffian framework of one (being) and many (beings), understanding being as pure, indeterminate stuff, the thing-in-itself, which although a prerequisite of knowing, is itself unknowable.[9] The picture we are left with is that we can know about finite beings, appear-

---

5. *ER*, 121.
6. Gilson, *Being*, 6, 25.
7. *ID*, 66.
8. Ibid., 52.
9. *ER*, 63; Gilson, *Being*, 134.

ances, but cannot even say anything about being qua being, as Aristotle had set out to do.

If one just cannot saying anything about being, ontological difference seems to hide the spectre of the very impossibility of ontology. A distinction of being from beings is presupposed to both charge that one avoids the question of being, and the claim some have made that being cannot even be an object of inquiry. We must briefly turn to Heidegger's explanation of how ontological difference arises, as a step towards understanding what he, in fact, means by this term.[10]

BEING AND DASEIN

Heidegger's employment of ontological difference parallels his distinction between the ontic and the ontological. Ontical truth has to do with how we ourselves are "situated." Ontical truth depends upon a certain way that we comport ourselves towards being. It is a certain disclosedness of being that makes possible beings. As Heidegger says, "The disclosedness of Being alone makes possible the manifestedness of being."[11] Heidegger is quick to clarify that the understanding of being that is not yet conceptualized can be termed "preontological." On the one hand we can speak of being as such. On the other hand, we have being as it is disclosed to Dasein, whereby through projection, thematization¾Dasein's situation¾and so on, a particular understanding of being emerges. The end result is that Dasein is left with an ontic realm, beings, and never just encounters being qua being. We are faced with ontological difference.

Heidegger claims that ontological difference is ground in the "transcendence of Dasein." Heidegger's basic approach is to show how the idea of ontological difference arises as a consequent to the very structure of Dasein. As he says: "For Dasein, to exist means to behave toward being while situated in the midst of being."[12] Upon a certain understanding of being Dasein can be said to have a world which would allow asking questions about it.[13]

Heidegger locates Dasein as the transcendental ground of ontological difference in that ontological truth allows for ontic truth. As Heidegger

10. BT, 2.
11. ER, 23.
12. Ibid., 115.
13. Ibid., 113.

says, "They belong together essentially, by reason of their relationship to the difference between Being and being (ontological difference). The essence of truth that must be bifurcated ontically and ontologically, is only possible given this difference."[14] Just as an understanding of being is presupposed or allows for any one being, the ontological difference gives rise to a dual notion of truth: the ontological and ontic.

Heidegger's approach can be termed transcendental, insofar as he took the ontological as fundamental. What is characteristic is that he will take the transcendental (ontological) grounds, as fundamental for the ontic.[15] Yet the ontological is inevitably understood in terms of Dasein.[16]

The salient features of Heidegger's genealogy of ontological difference are thus. Ontological difference, which seems to make a distinction of being from beings, is ground in Dasein. Furthermore, the ontological, understood in transcendental terms, provided the basis for ontic truths. Even here being and beings are in a reciprocal relationship insofar as ontological and ontic truth are. Being and beings are epistemologically co-dependent.

Heidegger quickly brings forth criticisms of Aristotle. The essential claim, again, is that Aristotle did not have an ontology. What is more interesting, however, is the reason. Aristotle, so says Heidegger, ends up dealing with ontical truths—in his four causes—while avoiding being qua being.

It will be by Heidegger's exploration and excavation of reason, that some light is shed on what he means by *ontological difference*, such to investigate one did not imply passing over the other.

LEIBNIZ AND REASON

Heidegger remarks that Leibniz formulated the principle of sufficient reason, which took some two thousand three hundred years.[17] The principle states, nothing is without reason. In positive terms, everything has a reason.[18] Heidegger wrote that there is a "history reigning in the long absence and sudden emergence of the principle of reason."[19]

14. Ibid., 27.
15. Ibid., 72–73.
16. Ibid., 123.
17. Ibid., 4–7.
18. *PR*, 5; *ER*, 11.
19. Ibid., 25.

In Leibniz's principle, reason equates with causality.[20] To ask the reason of something seems to mean, something like, "why is it here?" In causal terms, a reason for, say, the cup on the table is that I brought it there in order to have a drink. Heidegger wrote: "Leibniz obviously posits the principle of reason and the principle of causality as being equivalent."[21] Yet, as Heidegger also notes, not every reason is a cause. To say a bachelor is an unmarried man does not mean that a *bachelor* is the cause of being *unmarried*.

Although it is clear the principle of reason applies to this or that entity, it could also be applied to the totality of beings. It was indeed the logic of the principle of reason that would allow Leibniz to ask why something exists as opposed to nothing.[22] According to Heidegger, the principle of reason even becomes the fundamental principle of "rational cognition."[23] Since "everything has to be represented as a consequent," we ask the reason for any one representation. A representation counts as valid only if it corresponds to an object which is said to be its cause.[24]

What Heidegger exposed in his probing of the principle of sufficient reason, as proclaimed by Leibniz in the principium grande, the mighty principle, is that reason per se is being construed instrumentally. Reason is a way from moving from X to Y, whether understood as the relation of cause to an effect, means to an ends, or a premise to a conclusion in a syllogism. What we mean by asking for the reason of X, has a meaning that is different from Aristotle.

The principle of reason does not shed light upon how to understand ontological difference other than in terms of a radical divide between being and beings. In fact, the principle of sufficient reason seems to apply to beings alone, explaining, perhaps, the location of things (mass) in space-time in terms of causality along Newtonian lines. In short, the principle of reason seems to disclose ontic truths. If we kept asking the reason of any one thing, one would undoubtedly end up with an infinite regress. Heidegger used the principle of reason, as first formulated by Leibniz, as a point of departure, for tracking down being.

20. Ibid., 21.
21. Ibid.
22. Ibid., 27.
23. Ibid., 121.
24. Ibid., 27.

Part II: Interlude: Being and Ethics

REASON AND BEING

Heidegger considers *reason* in terms of *why*. Although *a reason* could be understood instrumentally, as either a cause, or justification for an epistemic claim, the *why* leads Heidegger beyond these employments. In fact, he reformulated Leibniz's principle as, "nothing is without a why."[25]

To understand what the *why* reveals we have to turn to Heidegger's reflection of a poem by Angelus Silesius, who wrote: "The rose is without a why, / it blooms because it blooms, / It pays no attention to itself, / asks not whether it is seen."[26] Heidegger's analysis of the poem has the following stages. First we are told that the rose is without a why; it has no reason. Second, we are told it blooms because it blooms. There is a reason for the blooming of the rose, which is nothing other than itself.

Third, the rose pays no attention to its grounds; it need not be aware of its why. Fourth, it does not care if anything else recognizes its ground. Heidegger goes on to point out, however, that if the poet merely wanted to distinguish the rose from humans he could a have said that the rose blooms because the sun shines.[27]

The "because" has a greater import than mere instrumental reason. Heidegger wrote, "The 'because' of the fragment simply points the blooming back to itself. The blooming is grounded in itself, it has its ground within itself."[28] The rose's *why* is not answered by appeal to anything outside of itself. Of the phrase "it blooms because it blooms," Heidegger wrote: "But this apparently vacuous talk . . . really says everything, namely everything there is to say here, doing so in its particular manner of not-speaking."[29] It would seem that *because* applies only to particular things, like the rose.

The principle of reason, Heidegger concludes, however, "proves to be not only a statement about beings; even more, what we bring into view is that the principle of reason speaks of the being of beings . . . What remains concealed is that it speaks of being." In fact, being has a kinship with reason, in that: "being in itself essentially comes to be a grounding."[30] The principle of reason, for Heidegger, has kinship to being, as both ground beings.

25. Ibid., 36.
26. Ibid., 36.
27. Ibid., 43.
28. Ibid., 57.
29. Ibid., 43.
30. Ibid., 49.

ONTOLOGICAL SIMILARITY

Although beings have a reason, being does not, as it is what grounds. Heidegger wrote, "Being can never first have a ground/reason which would supposedly ground it. Accordingly, ground/reason is missing from being ... To the extent that being as such grounds, it remains groundless. 'Being' does not fall within the orbit of the principle of reason, rather only beings do."[31] The principle reads, "nothing *is* without reason."

The important step that Heidegger took is to discuss being and reason in one breath. As he said, "The principle of reason speaks as a principle of being."[32] Heidegger noted that a "transformation," in our thinking is required to be able to equate both being and reason, and being and the abyss. In fact, Heidegger considers, "if the principle of reason is in truth a principle of being, if ground/reason and being say the same thing."[33] Although, he will not take them as identical, he will say, "Being and reason now ring out in unison."[34]

For clarification, first, "The shining of being is in play in the appearing of beings as soon as beings as such appear in their being."[35] Second, "Blooming is a pure arising on its own, a pure shining."[36] Structurally, there is something as the source of the shining, and an emanation of light outward. Heidegger wrote, "Being bestows itself, proffers itself to us in beings."[37] Being "furnishes the temporal play-space wherein beings can appear," said Heidegger.[38] Alluding to Leibniz, he said, "God plays and the world comes to be."[39] Heidegger also used the notion of *play* as to suggest the giving of being to beings.

We are also told however, "Compared to beings that are immediately accessible, being manifests the character of holding itself back, of concealing itself in a certain manner."[40] Whatever the relationship between being and beings, it still seems Heidegger regards ontological difference as

---

31. Ibid., 51.
32. Ibid., 52.
33. Ibid., 56.
34. Ibid., 125.
35. Ibid., 54.
36. Ibid., 57.
37. Ibid., 54.
38. Ibid., 62.
39. Ibid., 112–13.
40. Ibid., 63.

suggesting two conceptually distinct categories, which can be misleading to the extent it covers up their ontological kinship.

The why or reason of beings is being, which stands as their ultimate ground. Heidegger tells us, in fact, that we can hear the principle of reason in two ways. We can hear it as the principle of beings or being. Yet Heidegger noted that when we think of the principle of reason "we are pointed towards thinking ground/reason as being and being as ground/reason. When this is the case we begin trying to think being qua being."[41]

The path to being, according to Heidegger, is to hear "the principle of reason as a principle of being."[42] The principle of reason, first thought in connection to beings, particular things, with a "leap," and a change in intonation, "allow a unison between being and reason to resound," as they belong "together."[43] When Heidegger said that being and reason belong together, he is not claiming they are identical, as if one could merely use the words interchangeably; rather, he claims they are held together.

According to Heidegger, the destiny of being has led behind a trail, such as we find in the ways in which we have understood *ground/reason*. We have understood beings in terms of ratio, cause, and as the principle of sufficient reason, and not as "a letting-lie-present that assembles."[44]

Being, according to Heidegger, is what grounds, yet itself has no grounds.[45] We could say, although beings have a reason, being has no reason as that which "allows beings to be beings."[46] Yet, due to the formulation of the principle of sufficient reason by Leibniz—everything has a reason—we even seek a ground for being. But, as already stated, being does not have a reason. Heidegger made a similar point in relation to the "because." Heidegger wrote: "For the 'because' is without 'why,' it has no ground, it is ground itself."[47] The "because" points to the essence of being, according to Heidegger.

In considering the relationship between reason/ground and being, we have moved closer, said Heidegger, to what is worth thinking about. Indeed, for Heidegger, what is worthy of thought is the essence of being,

41. Ibid., 68.
42. Ibid.
43. Ibid., 89–90.
44. Ibid., 110.
45. Ibid., 111.
46. Ibid., 125.
47. Ibid., 126–27.

and not merely "the recklessness of calculative thinking and its immense achievements."⁴⁸

Insofar as being is present in particular things, there is a kinship between the (1) reason of a particular thing and (2) reason per se. The consequence is that being and beings are co-dependent. Heidegger wrote, "Not only does Being ground beings as their ground, but beings in their turn ground, cause Being in their own way. Beings can do so only insofar as they 'are' the fullness of Being: they are what is most of all."⁴⁹ Heidegger is able to unite being and beings by allowing reason to be both universal and particular.

Everything seems to hang on this: "It depends on whether the force of the claim of the 'why' submits to the enabling appeal of the 'because.'"⁵⁰ If we recall the poem by Silesius, the "because" is supposed to suggest a reason for the blooming of the rose, which, as it happens, is nothing other than the activity itself. The principle of sufficient reason leads Heidegger to being. For him, "The appeal of the word of being speaks in the principle of reason."⁵¹

Seeing that the reason for beings is being, the ontological divided is united by reason. Anything, like a rose, does not find its reason as a means to an end beyond itself, but in being what it is: It blooms because it blooms; its reason does not lie outside of itself either. The rose's reason lies incipient within itself. Reason *is*.⁵² Reason, like being, is common to each thing.

ESSENCE AND REASON

Grieder, a commentator interested in Heidegger's medieval roots, remarks on connecting reason to being: "As is well known, Heidegger insisted on the ontological difference, the fundamental distinction between beings and Being. Yet he speaks both of the Essence of beings and the Essence of Being, a fact which is puzzling."⁵³

---

48. Ibid., 129.
49. *ID*, 68–69.
50. *PR*, 128.
51. Ibid.
52. Heidegger wrote, "The Being of beings means Being which is being" (*Identity and Difference*, 64).
53. Grieder, "What Did Heidegger Mean," 84.

Part II: Interlude: Being and Ethics

Essence, recall, is used by Heidegger in relation to beings and being. That is to say, the problem emerged for Grieder that if Heidegger is going to maintain a radical distinction of beings from being, how are they mutually exclusive. But is Heidegger committed to ontological difference, anyways? In Heidegger's later writings, like "The Origin of the Work of Art," he has already referred to ontological difference as a "problem."[54]

Indeed, it can well be said that the exploration of *reason/ground/essence* is at least one strategy Heidegger employs to pursue being. To comprehend how *essence* is supposed to bridge the gap of beings from being requires discerning what Heidegger meant by it.

At first glance, essence, reinforces an ontological distinction. We assume that essences have being and are eternal in nature but lack the existence of particular things that are subject to change and time.[55] The essence/existence distinction within the framework of ontological difference. As Knasas, a medieval scholar, said, "Heidegger appears to regard the essence/existence distinction among the Scholastics as simply an ad hoc device fashioned to distinguish creatures from God."[56] God is being, and the creation is constituted by beings.

According to Kahn, another scholar interested in the historical nature of Heidegger's being question, however, it would only be with biblical influence that one could conceive of the world as an idea in the mind of God, where existence is something He imparts to creation. Even Gilson concurs:

> "Averroes was right at least in this, that the origin of the notion of existence, as distinct from the notion of essence, is religious and tied up with the notion of creation . . . [creatures] receive their existence from God . . . In short, the distinction between creatures and their Creator entails, in creatures themselves, a distinction between their existence and the essence of their being.[57]

The idea of ontological difference—as conceived as a distinction of being from beings, God from creation—finds an expression in the relationship between an essence to an existing thing.[58] We move from God, to essences unto existing beings.

---

54. *PLT*, 86.
55. Kahn, "Why Existence," 7.
56. Knasas, "Heideggerian Critique," 435.
57. Gilson, *Being*, 62–63.
58. Ibid., 214.

Yet ontological difference remains, as we distinguish the one and the many. The only plausible way to go beyond a distinction of beings from being, as Gilson remarks, is "through overcoming all essences without ever losing them, to reach their common source, itself beyond essences yet containing them all."[59] There is reason to think that Heidegger, more generally, does get to being, without losing the world.

First of all, it is not clear what it would mean to investigate being completely divorced from beings. Second, to address beings does not mean require passing over being. For Heidegger, to seek the reason, ground or essence—the why?—of any one being is to find a hint to the meaning of being.[60]

Ontological difference entails a distinction between being and beings. As Heidegger notes, "beings are always individually occurring beings and thus multifarious; contrary to this, being is unique, the absolute singular in unconditioned singularity."[61] He also said, "Thus we think Being rigorously only when we think of it in its difference with beings, and of beings in their difference with Being."[62]

Brentano, arguably, first introduced Heidegger to the problem of ontological difference in his dissertation on Aristotle. He points out that, for Aristotle, being is what is most general.[63] However, according to Brentano, for Aristotle, substance is a being first in concept, cognition, and time.[64] Although we could, as Aristotle did, study being by way of beings evades dealing with the fundamental object of ontology.[65] As Gilson notes, since Aristotle defined ontology as a distinct science, it was supposed to deal with being qua being.[66]

---

59. Ibid., 208.

60. Heidegger wrote, "Hints only remain hints when thinking does not twist them into definitive statements and thereby come to a standstill with them. Hints are hints only as long as thinking follows their allusions while meditating on them. Thus, thinking reaches a path that leads to what has from time immemorial shown itself in the tradition of our thinking as worth of thought, and simultaneously veils itself" (PR, 129).

61. PR, 84.

62. ID, 62.

63. Brentano, *Several Senses*, 1–3.

64. Ibid., 148.

65. In Gilson, *Being*, 74.

66. Ibid., 1.

Part II: Interlude: Being and Ethics

As Heidegger remarked, Aristotle attempts to do ontology is by way of first causes.[67] To know what a substance is, requires answering the *why* of that thing. The reason of a thing is explained by a thing's *telos*—what it is intended to be. Aristotle's causes, more generally, are supposed to answer what a being is, the fact that it is, and its being true.

Heidegger begins his meditation on reason with Aristotle, which meant discerning the four causes.[68] A substance's essence is its *why*. The essence applies to an entire type, *houseness*, or *personness*.[69] Not only how an essence causes a thing is obscure, but we are still dealing with beings (many essences) and not being.[70] According to Heidegger, the four causes still fall prey to the charge of forgetfulness of being.

For Heidegger, ontological difference is an outcome of the structure of Dasein. Even here, however, where being and beings are distinguished, they are still in an epistemological relationship: beings are consequent to an interpretation of being.

Recall, for Aristotle, to understand what a thing is required grasping its *telos*. In Aristotle's terms, efficient causality would come to reign supreme in Leibniz's principle of sufficient reason. The history of reason does not just retain the Aristotelian meaning. That is to say, as the principle of reason, one would always be thinking in terms of a cause. In Leibniz's formulation of the principle of sufficient reason, Heidegger is able to uncover the way reason is construed in efficient, causal terms.

Heidegger did insist that ontological difference was ground in the structure of Dasein, as found in *The Essence of Reasons*. Yet his further reflection upon reason, in *The Principle of Reason* erodes it. For Heidegger, being particularizes itself in individual things, like the rose.

He is clear to point out that being and reason are not the same, but, "Being and reason now ring out in unison."[71] The reason, ground, or essence of beings, and being, we are told, ring out in unison, belong together, and are held together.[72] The *because* of the rose could be said to be both particular (to that rose) and universal (as being). The difference of being

---

67. Ibid., 160.
68. Ibid., 157.
69. Ibid., 159.
70. *ER*, 5; Knasas, "Heideggerian Critique," 425.
71. *PR*, 125.
72. Ibid., 89–90.

from beings does not disappear, as Heidegger said, "We follow it to its essential origin."[73]

"The rose blooms because it blooms" exposes a double meaning. On the one hand the rose blooms because of itself, not because it was watered, received sunshine and so on. The cause of the rose's blooming is its blooming. On the other hand, *because* is universal. *Because* applies to a particular thing, and all of them. It is common to the opposite poles of ontological difference.

Although we can conceptually separate one-being from many-beings, ontologically they are not mutually exclusive. Reason as being (which is one), simultaneously serves as the ground/reason of particular beings (the many). In this way being pervades beings. Ontological difference, for Heidegger, implied a similitude of beings and being. Fallenness, ironically, is to cling to a radical understanding of *ontological difference*, where beings and being are mutually exclusive. Insofar as Dasein must abide by ontological difference, since the fissure with being occurred, we are fallen.

We are separated¾by an abyss. Heidegger, so the charge goes, is not a mystic at all. I argued in this chapter that if we do not read Heidegger as a mystic we are left clueless about how to understand the question concerning the meaning of being. Caputo said that Heidegger's question leads nowhere.[74] Heidegger, I submit, mitigated radical ontological difference, by collapsing the dichotomy between beings and being. Evading radical ontological difference throws the doors open to mysticism.

First, the mystical element in Heidegger's thought, as Caputo, dubbed it, in the title of his book by the same name, has received attention by scholars.[75] Coupled with Heidegger's own pronouncements, it is problematic to read him as a mystic. Heidegger's critique of onto-theology, after all, is a criticism of the notion that we spring from a divine ground.

Safranski wrote, "And the question about Being did not ask for some supreme being that at one time used to be called God; instead the question is designed to create the distance that permits us to experience this relation."[76] The "distance" is the sine qua non of the Heideggerian predicament: To be so far from the nearest.

---

73. *ID*, 62–65.
74. Caputo, *Demythologizing Heidegger*.
75. Caputo, *Mystical Element*; Sikka, *Forms of Transcendence*.
76. Safranski, *Martin Heidegger*, 307.

Part II: Interlude: Being and Ethics

Second, in his "Letter on Humanism," indicating radical ontological difference, Heidegger talks of man as the Sheppard of being. In an interesting study of Hegel's philosophy, however, Williamson made distinctions that may be helpful to entangle ourselves from the Sheppard remark.[77] Williamson distinguished pantheism from panentheism, which are two ways to collapse ontological difference. A pantheist believes that God is no different from the world. Panentheism, however, is the view that God exists in all beings.

In dissolving radical ontological difference, Heidegger is a pantheist if he renders being and beings equivalencies. For a pantheist, "we are the shepherd of being" is figurative (as there no difference between God and the shepherd). Heidegger is a panentheist if he thinks being pervades beings. For the panentheist, we can be Sheppard's in a literal sense (having to tend to the God-relationship). Suffice it to say, Heidegger may be read as a pantheist or panentheist. It has been my purpose is to suggest the plausibility of a mystical reading of Heidegger's opus, not to develop it, which goes beyond the scope of this book.[78] Reading Heidegger as a mystic is at least one way of making sense out of the question of being.

At the very least, we do not have to abandon Heidegger's call that we look to the being-relationship as the foundation of ethics. Heidegger's reading of the tradition explains in detail what happens when we lose our correct relationship to being. It is of little surprise, then, that our ethical lights will be illuminated only when, according to him, this relationship to the ground of Dasein is restored. What is left to be done is draw out what this relationship could mean for ethics. Given that Heidegger has said scant little about ethics, it is by way of comparisons and contrasts I suggest we seek to draw out the details, to which I turn to in the next part.

---

77. Williamson, *Introduction to Hegel's*, 234.
78. Sikka, *Forms of Transcendence*.

PART III

Contrasts and Reflections

7

Kant's Conundrum

I considered Heidegger's reading of a Kantian ethic in chapter 1; in this chapter, I examine in further detail how Heidegger builds an ethics from his reading of Kant. For Kant, what *ought to be* is justified by appeal to metaphysical concepts, such as God. Yet Kant had banned the use of notions such as God and freedom in the first critique. For Kant, furthermore, the *justification* of ethics—doing God's will—can serve no role in *motivating* ethical behavior.

Yet according to Heidegger, we were to look carefully at why we act ethically, we would discover that at base lies a justification that is also the original motivation for ethics. Heidegger challenges the notion that we must separate, as Kant does, motivation from duty, ethics from nature, and, more generally, practice from theory.

KANT'S GRAND THEORY

Though Kant conceded that metaphysics is of little value for practical action, he contends that it is "not useless . . . to investigate metaphysics as the first ground of the doctrine of virtue."[1] What Kant has in mind is first gleaned by what he excludes. No moral principle, according to Kant, is based on feeling.[2] Nor can the moral law be based on external rewards, such as happiness, (which though entailed, he said, can only be fully re-

1. *FMM*, 181–82.
2. Ibid., 182.

alized in eternity).³ Nor can the moral law be based on external threats (such as those sometimes found in religions).⁴

Morality, for Kant, deals exclusively with what comes from the inside, the will. He thinks that the duty to love is absurd (because it involves feelings, not the will). In fact, freedom of the will, according to Kant, entails the overcoming (*Überwildung*) of inclination by reason. Even rights, which deals with an external law giver, he tells us, must accord with the moral law, not feeling or conscience.⁵ He, furthermore, located our dignity in conjunction with the will; for example, he says that it is an affront to our dignity to bow down before anything.⁶

For Kant, ethics deals with "the relation of men to men," and did not apply to the relationship between man and God, which "goes completely beyond the bounds of ethics."⁷ The will must rely upon itself, not, for instance, God. As he puts it, "Man's greatest moral perfection is to do his duty from duty (for the law to be not only the rule but also the incentive of his actions)."⁸ Kant discerns the basis of morality thus:

> Moral self-knowledge, which seeks to penetrate into the depths (the abyss) of one's heart that are quite difficult to fathom, is the beginning of all human wisdom. For in the case of man, the ultimate wisdom, which consists in the harmony of one's being with its final end, requires him first to remove the obstacle within (an evil will actually present in him) and then to develop the original predisposition to a good will within him, which can never be lost. (Only descent into the hell of self-knowledge can pave the way to godliness).⁹

Since Kant set out to place limitations on what can be known, and develop a system of *a priori* knowledge from concepts, it would seem that, first, ethics cannot rest on metaphysics, that is, what is unknowable, and second, it must be derived *a priori* from concepts.¹⁰ Since he distinguished a

---

3. *FMM*, 183; *CPR*, 115, 133.
4. *FMM*, 272.
5. *FMM*, 185; *CPR*, 74, 85.
6. *FMM*, 232.
7. Ibid., 279.
8. Ibid., 196.
9. Ibid., 236.
10. *CPR*, Axx.

rational finite being from an infinite one, all of knowledge must be justified without appeal to what we cannot comprehend.

Yet Kant also talks of the highest good, the best of all possible worlds, which we cannot even comprehend if it requires measuring our world against infinite alternative ones. Still, Kant assumed a number of concepts, like transcendental freedom, God, and immortality.[11]

Our duty is determined by the Kantian thought experiment, in which we are to consider if we could assent to behavior *P* if all people acted likewise in situation *S*. The practical (duty) and theoretical (the highest good) require going beyond what we could reasonably account for in practice.

To justify the notion that duty leads to the highest good, he wrote, "Therefore it is morally necessary to assume the existence of God."[12] God, he is clear to point out, is not necessary for all moral obligations, but more generally, so that we have a duty to promote the highest good, and we cannot, he said, conceives of the highest good without the highest intelligence.[13] The relationship between duty and the highest good, he calls, "a hypothesis, i.e., a ground for explanation."[14] Duty to the highest good, he said, is pure rational faith.[15] By abiding by the moral law, single-mindedly devoted to by rational agents, he said, we "bring the kingdom of God to us."[16]

According to Kant, it is through the highest good that pure practical reason leads to religion, that is, recognition of duties of divine commandments.[17] We can, he said, hope for the highest good only from a morally perfect and omnipotent will.[18]

For Kant, morality, however, does not deal with happiness but what it is to be worthy of happiness.[19] We are worthy of happiness when we are in accord with the highest good.[20] Though Kant thinks the moral law is holy,

---

11. Ibid., 100, 130, 133.
12. Ibid., 130.
13. Ibid.
14. Ibid.
15. Ibid.
16. Ibid., 133, 135.
17. Ibid., 134.
18. Ibid.
19. Ibid.
20. Ibid., 135.

yet notes, "He [God] is the only holy, the only blessed, the only wise being, because these terms imply unlimitedness."[21]

For practical reason to be effective in obtaining the highest good, the postulates of theoretical reason (God, immorality, freedom) are "assumed." (see Table 2, "Kant's Ethical Theory")[22] God guarantees one's eternal reward, making it the best of all possible worlds. Only God, being omniscient, further, could judge if it was the best of all possible worlds.[23] Also, in the best of all possible worlds, freedom is required to have a pure will.

Table 2
"Kant's Ethical Theory"

Practical motivation		Theoretical postulates		Consequence
Self	Duty	Highest good	God	Happiness in eternity

Duty entails accordance with the highest good, which is guaranteed by God.[24] Kant contends that the concept of God belongs to morals not speculation.[25] It is God that makes possible the conditions for the best of all possible worlds that includes freedom and immortality.[26]

Kant tells us, it is God that has so configured the world as to implant the intention to do the good, which will result in the best of all possible worlds.[27] Kant wants us to act, employing practical reason, legislating, as it were.

Though evidence for God, according to Kant, is the moral order, it is an "adornment" of the world, as well as nature.[28] Whereas, for example, nature is given, we actualize the kingdom of ends.[29] The God postulate is necessary for morality, but not for physics.[30] Ethics must be actualized by

---

21. Ibid., 136.
22. Ibid., 139.
23. Ibid., 143.
24. Ibid., 144.
25. Ibid., 145.
26. Ibid., 148.
27. Ibid.
28. *FMM*, 270.
29. *CPR*, 151.
30. Ibid., 143.

human freedom. Kant is impressed by both scientific knowledge (the starry sky above) and moral knowledge (the moral law within).[31]

For Kant, nature and morality are united as constituents of the best of all possible worlds. Morality has a final end (individually for myself) and collectively (by contributing to highest good). Our ethical motivation must always be, for Kant, duty, which is an allegiance of our will to do the good.

THE GROUND OF ETHICS

Bernard Williams, who teaches at All Souls College, Oxford, in an important study, *Ethics and the Limits of Philosophy*, scrutinized the foundation on which Kant wants to rest his ethics. Williams claimed that Kant did not focus on developing an account of the good life, but "offers certain structural or formal features of ethical relations . . . it starts from the very abstract conception of rational agency."[32] As Williams explained, Kant cannot offer a foundation for ethics because any reason would be moral or non-moral.[33] If a reason was non-moral, however, it cannot be the motivation of ethics. For Kant, we may wish to recall, morality cannot be rendered dependent upon external considerations, like the highest good, or for God. Yet, a moral reason to be ethical would lead to circularity. Williams commented, Kant's thought that we could come to understand why morality should rightly be present itself to the rational agent as a categorical demand. It was because rational agency itself involved accepting such a demand, and this is why Kant described morality in terms of laws laid down by practical reason itself."[34]

Yet, Williams wrote, "Why should I think of myself as a legislator and—since there is no distinction—at the same time a citizen of a republic governed by these natural laws? The [Kantian] argument needs to tell us what it is about rational agents that requires them to form this conception of themselves as, so to speak, abstract citizens."[35]

---

31. Ibid., 166.
32. B. Williams, *Ethics and the Limits of Philosophy*, 54.
33. Ibid., 55.
34. Ibid.
35. Ibid., 63.

William concluded, "There is no route to the impartial standpoint from deliberation alone."[36] Rather, Williams contended, we must start with ethical experience itself.[37]

Peter Singer, an Oxonian and modern day utilitarian, who teaches at Princeton University, noted the question—why should I act morally?—is a question about ethics per se. The question is tantamount to asking why I should adopt an ethical point of view, which he took to be a concern with the interests of others.[38] Singer considered the case of the psychopath, since it is an example of someone who seems incapable of considering the interest of others. The psychopath is an example of where personal happiness and ethics do not coincide.[39] Singer further suggested that to adopt the ethical point of view required thinking life is meaningful. He concluded: "'Why act morally?' cannot be given an answer that will provide everyone with overwhelming reasons for acting morally. Ethically indefensible behaviour is not always irrational. We will probably always need the sanctions of the law and social pressure to provide additional reasons against serious violations of ethical standards."[40]

Here lies Kant's conundrum. He cannot find the foundation of ethics in nature or God, but he cannot find it within reason, either. The psychologist is perhaps bound to fall prey to the naturalistic fallacy, the idea that we can reduce the good to natural properties like "pleasant" or "desirable." The naturalistic fallacy is consistent with Kant's concern that in forming an ethics we must separate what motivates it from what justifies it. Yet if we avoid the pitfall of explaining ethics by way of our motivations, we likely succumb to, what I have dubbed the unnatural fallacy of attempting to ground ethical values on something other than a biological account of human nature. Yet because of the deficiencies in Kant's standard account made plain by Williams, it is a psychological tack which we are prompted to consider next.

Piaget in *The Moral Development of the Child* articulated a cognitive view of moral development that in outline supports the Kantian outlook, though using terms (e.g., "duty") in his own manner. Piaget articulated how we acquire physical laws in terms of regularity of experiences, which he extended to morality. According to Piaget, "Duty is nothing more than

---

36. Ibid., 70.
37. Ibid., 91.
38. Singer, *Practical Ethics*, 202, 204.
39. Ibid., 215–16.
40. Ibid., 220.

acceptance of commands received from without."[41] We follow rules, which we internalize as our own.

He also thought mutual respect is the basis of intellectual and moral autonomy. Piaget distinguished coercion (unilateral respect) from cooperation (mutual respect). As he put it, "For moral autonomy appears when the mind regards as necessary an ideal that is independent of all external pressures."[42] He went on, "Now, apart from our relations to other people, there can be no moral necessity."[43]

Autonomy appears only with reciprocity, when mutual respect is strong enough the individual feels from within the desire to treat others as he himself would wish to be treated.[44]

In psychological development he observed three seminal phases: (1) 7 to 8 years, justice is subordinate to adult authority; (2) 8 to 11 years, progressive equalitarianism; (3) 11 to 12 years, purely equalitarian justice is tempered with considerations for equality. True justice, he told us, depends on free consent. Commenting on the primitive mode of existence Piaget wrote,

> The kernel of these beliefs [i.e., the duties that hold society together] is the feeling of the sacred, the source of all morality and religion. Whatever offends against these powerful feelings is crime, and all crime is 'sacrilege.'[45]

Mirroring this theory of moral development, Piaget distinguished the primitive, rule-based (collective) from advanced conscience-based (individualistic) societies. The child and primitive respects authority, but the adult and modern dweller, according to Piaget, is able to relate to the other with mutual respect, which "provokes a spontaneous longing."[46]

According to Singer and Williams, there is nothing inherent in being rational that will require us to take on the ethical point of view. Piaget's account of the development of morality can potentially break the dichotomy between other- and self-interest. For Piaget, concern for the interests of others arises in a situation of mutual respect.

41. Piaget, *Moral Judgement*, 106.
42. Ibid., 196.
43. Ibid.
44. Ibid.
45. Ibid., 330.
46. Ibid., 355. Further, according to Piaget, cooperation as the basis of mature morals is consistent with the freedom required to search for the truth.

In fact, Heidegger interprets the Kantian kingdom of ends in terms of a situation where self-interest and that of others does not conflict. To be self-interested, at least, does not without further explanation, as Kant thought, indicate unethical behavior.

In fact duty is never as pure as Kant made it out to be. Kantian duty required acting as if one was legislating a moral law. We are at least hypothetically considering an external consequence—namely, the situation in which all people could accord with acts of our will. Heidegger offers a remedy to criticisms of Kant, like those of Williams and Singer. He blurs the distinction between motivation and justification.

According to Heidegger, we cannot distinguish between practical and theoretical and reason in the first place. That is, attempting to distinguish, as Kant does, between practical and theoretical reason based on the fact that we deal with a finite being, on the one hand, and on the other, unlimited concepts, is dubious. The upshot is that the theoretical component—aiming at the highest good—is required to motivate practical reason—duty. Further, as Piaget suggested, we can only aim at goods beyond ourselves because at some point in the developmental process we are exposed to a situation involving mutual respect or at least empathy.

As I have already suggested, a Heideggerian ethic yields an orientation towards the world. Notice, Singer buoys up the idea that at the base of ethics we require an outlook, for example, that human existence is meaningful.

I considered several attempts to say something about what a fundamental relationship to being may look like, which have sublime aspects. I have not, admittedly, however, said much about the nature of the sublime. The sublime is recognition of something like Kant's kingdom of ends, which is a harmony between us and everything else. It could even be an experience of the grotesque nature of war, a negative sublime, which may also give rise to sympathy with beings. The sublime could be understood in Kantian terms of aesthetic judgement. Generally, with the sublime, we are usually speaking of an experience that is so overwhelming that it reorients us. The sublime, to motive an ethics, requires a submission of our will to our recognition.

The direction I want to pursue differs from Schalow's emphasis, discussed in chapter 2, upon the imagination. I propose, rather, that a certain sublime experience of the world is required to serve as the bedrock of a

Heideggerian ethic.[47] The sublime experience is yielded by a fundamental relationship to being.

We need not, of course, require that we all experience the sublime in order to be ethical. Much of ethical knowledge may be a matter of habit or education. To ask for the foundation of ethics, recall, is to seek where it ultimately finds its footing, and it is that which, I have suggested, for Heidegger, rests upon the experience of the sublime.

We may wish to question if Heidegger gets Kant right. Yet if we grant Heidegger's reading of Kant, as a heuristic for developing his own view, we are rewarded with unique results. Most importantly for my purposes, Heidegger's reading undermines Williams' denial that a feeling could not be the basis of Kant's ethics.

Heidegger perceived a fall from grace. He wished to rest ethics on metaphysics. Yet what that metaphysics consists in, and its relation to ethics changes in Heidegger's appropriation of Kant. As we have seen, Heidegger emphasized the motivational feeling of Kantain ethics, respect (*Auchtung*), not duty (*Dienst*). I suggest that Heidegger took the emphasis upon the motivation of ethics one step further by linking it to his being-relationship, which culminated in letting beings be.

The main problem that confronts us lies is saying something about what letting beings be amounts to. Talking of avoiding the Kantian formalism is intriguing. Yet I need to provide an example of a Heideggerian ethics. Yet we must also still confront the problem of proposing a Heideggerian ethic that is platitudinous.

In Genesis, we are evicted from the garden of Eden. The Romantics and, in Germany, the Idealists take up the idea of a fall from grace.[48] The loss of Eden is not fatal, however. Ethics, for Kant, required actualizing the way things ought to be; so too, for Heidegger. In chapter 8, as an illustration of the Heideggerian aim of letting beings be, I shall consider how Hegel links ethics to aesthetics.

---

47. Schalow, *Imagination and Existence*, 299.
48. *FMM*, 15.

8

Hegel's Aesthetics

In writing "Poetry is man's original grasp of the truth,"[1] G. W. F. Hegel precedes Heidegger's concern with poetry and language, romantic idealism, and, later on, the idea of destiny. It is to Hegel's thought on aesthetics we now turn to look into an aesthetic ethic, where feelings are emphasized.

I have been preoccupied with the idea that a Heideggerian ethics must be founded upon emotions. One place where emotions are indispensible are in our appreciation of the arts. Specifically, I shall attempt to show how by looking to Hegel's thought on aesthetics we can avoid global relativism, allowing us to further refine a possible trajectory of Heidegger's thinking.

DESCARTES, SPINOZA, AND KANT: THE SUBJECTIVITY OF THE ARTS

The idea that would come to the fore in the sixteenth century was that beauty was to be determined based on our mechanical reactions to pleasure and pain, as we find in Descartes' *Passions of the Soul* and Spinoza's *Ethics*. Kant extended the rationalists' scrutiny of the emotions to reason. And in his *Critique of the Power of Judgement*, Kant aimed to explain how we make aesthetic judgements based on his theory of mind. Let us start in France.

Descartes' writings mark a systematic and mathematically oriented view of the world, but applied to all domains of inquiry. According to Descartes, first, actions and passions are always "a single thing"; and second,

---

1. *PFA*, 145.

everything in us can be traced to back to our body or soul.² He distinguishes between what is as "suitable" (hence, love) and that which is "harmful" (hence, hated).³

Desire, he claims, is the aim to preserve what is good and avoid that which can do us harm. Further, Descartes is clear to point out that love and hatred can be related to usefulness and harm to the body, but not the soul. In fact, he distinguished two varieties of both love and hatred, those with the senses (the beautiful and ugly), and those resting in reason (the good and bad). As he put it, in Article 85, titled "About Abhorrence and Delight," "For we commonly call good and evil what our internal senses or our reason makes us judge suitable or opposed to our nature, but we call beautiful and ugly what is so represented to us by our external senses."

For Descartes, subjectivity lies with the senses and objectivity with reason. We make judgements about what we love and hate, but some have "ordinarily less truth" and "deceive," while others are more the providence of reason, and hence truth.⁴ Specifically, art merely concerns our subjective likes and dislikes; ethics, however, is about what is right and wrong ascertained by the application of reason.

Spinoza's account of beauty can be gleaned from his *Ethics*, which is primarily a treatise on metaphysics. Spinoza complained that all Descartes did in his analysis of the passions was show the "keenness of his intellect."⁵ Yet Spinoza echoed many of the same ideas that take hold in Descartes thought by rooting aesthetic appreciation in biology and, then, separating that from the providence of reason. According to Spinoza, everything we do is because it is considered "useful."⁶ He argued, however, that the ignorant consider things good or bad merely by how they are affected by it in the present. He went on, "As brains differ, so do tastes."⁷

---

2. *PS*, 1, a. 1; 1, a. 7. In referencing Descartes here, the first numeral indicates the part of that text followed by the article: for example, "1, a. 7" is Part I, article 7.

3. *PS*, 2, a. 56.

4. Ibid., 2, a. 85.

5. *E*, 3, Preface. For Spinoza's *Ethics*, the first numeral indicates the part of that text followed by "D," Definition; "P," Proposition; or "S," *Scholium* (and sometimes a further specification, like "Appendix" that is self-explanatory): so, for instance, "2P40S2" is Part II, Proposition 40, Scholium 2.

6. Ibid., 1P36, Appendix.

7. Ibid., 1P36, Appendix.

According to Spinoza, we hate what causes us "pain" and love that which gives us "pleasure."[8] In fact, he defined love as pleasure accompanied by the idea of an "external object."[9] Emotions are for him "confused ideas."[10]

For Spinoza, the good that is really "useful to us," and the bad that will actually "hinder us from possessing the good" is just an "awareness of pleasure and pain," determined with an eye to the "future."[11] Knowledge of good and bad give rise to the desire to overcome other emotions; the good and bad are stronger experiences of "pleasure and pain."[12]

In sum, according to Spinoza, all actions of reason are good. Our goal is to perfect reason because it leads to "knowledge of God," supreme happiness, and helps us avoid the "excess" of our inferior emotions.[13] Spinoza's prioritizes reason over the emotions in the rational person. According to him, emotions let us distinguish what we love from what we hate based on pleasure and pain in the short term. Reason, however, allows us to distinguish what is good or bad, pleasurable and painful. As with Descartes, the arts are likely subjective, while reason allows us to refine our emotions, in this case thinking of how our acts will impact us in the long term.

Kant takes up the schism whereby reason is a reliable indicator of truth and the senses are not in a more sophisticated way than Descartes or Spinoza; he calls into question the power of reason itself that is presupposed as apodictic by the earlier rationalist thinkers. Specifically, he internalizes universals as, for instance, the categories of the mind, while particulars are a consequence to judgements rendered by it. It is important to consider Kant's thought because he provides the putative claim of the subjectivity of the arts that was often the direct object of Hegel's critique.

Topographically, Kant's three main works can be distinguished between a concern with science and theory, on the one hand, the *Critique of Pure Reason*, from, on the other, its practical counterparts, like ethics, the *Critique of Practical Reason*, and the arts, the *Critique of the Power of Judgement*.[14]

---

8. Ibid., 3P17, Demonstration.
9. Ibid., 3P30S.
10. Ibid., 3, General Definitions of the Emotions.
11. Ibid., 4D1–2; 4P8, 16.
12. Ibid., 4P19.
13. Ibid., 4P28, Appendix.
14. *CPJ*, 20:196.

In Kant's writings, we encounter a division that cuts through all of his thought, bearing upon his aesthetics and bringing with it the mechanistic presuppositions that were germane to the scientific revolutions of his day. For Kant we understand universals (theory) and make judgements about particulars (practice).

All faculties of the mind, for Kant, can be traced to (a) the faculty of cognition, (b) the feeling of pleasure or displeasure, and (c) the faculty of desire that concerns final ends. To determine the beauty of an object, for Kant, we do not relate it to cognition but, rather, as a possible feeling of pleasure or displeasure, which means that it cannot be "other than subjective."[15] Yet at the same time he denies that what is beautiful is only so for "me."[16]

As Kant said, "By right, only production through freedom, i.e., a capacity for choice that grounds its actions in reason, should be called art."[17] So Kant brings art within the scope of rational thought. However, making a distinction from beauty that alone can be applied to nature, Kant called the sublime a "negative feeling" because it creates a kind of displeasure.[18] While both beauty and the sublime, he said, please as an end, the later is related to reason and exhausts its abilities. Beauty deals with "quality" and the sublime "quantity."[19] For Kant, the sublime is the "absolutely great."[20] As Kant put it, "That is sublime which even to be able to think of demonstrates a faculty of mind that surpasses every measure of the senses ... which determines the mind to think of the unattainability of nature as the presentation of ideas."[21]

For Kant, however, we cannot know nature's final ends through the mind, and so from a practical point of view, we must conceive of God as "a regulative principle for our actions."[22] The sublime, elicited by the greatest works of art, in Kant's thought is the feeling that indicates our epistemic limitations.

---

15. Ibid., 5:204.
16. Ibid., 5:213.
17. Ibid., 5:303.
18. Ibid., 5:245.
19. *CPJ*, 5:247.
20. Ibid., 5:248.
21. Ibid., 5:250, 5:268.
22. Ibid., 5:453.

Part III: Contrasts and Reflections

From the conspectus on Kant, we can take away the following. Art cannot be a vehicle for truth, as Hegel claimed, because art is even more removed from matters of truth because its appraisal rests on its ability to affect in us pleasure or displeasure. At best, we can speak of the universality of aesthetic judgement insofar as we all share a consensual reaction to a work of art.

In providing historical vignettes of Descartes,' Spinoza's, and Kant's thought, I have glossed over differences between them in order to bring out how each separated the passions from reason and the consequence of doing so. Namely, art is thought of by both Descartes and Spinoza as subjective because it is rooted in our emotional reactions; ethics is less relative because it requires rational refinement of our passions, by requiring judgements about what is healthy, good, and harmful, evil (Descartes), or similarly useful or not so in the long term (Spinoza). For these thinkers in the case of ethics, but not the arts, we can make wrong judgements, so there is an objective fact of the matter beyond our own impressions.

Since the separation between what is emotional and rational can be disputed, it is not surprising Kant brings both aesthetics and ethics (in fact the whole of knowledge) within the purview of intersubjective knowledge. We leave aside Kant's view of knowledge, because it takes us beyond the scope of this discussion of the arts. The moral is that once we separate the mind from the body, and epistemologically privilege reason as a source of knowledge, it was only a matter of time till both aesthetics and ethics fall by the realist's wayside.

The upshot is that it is difficult to see how, according to Descartes or Spinoza, temporal artefacts that cause us pleasure in the present could lead to knowledge. With Spinoza, however, the door is left open to aesthetic realism, the idea that beauty can be discovered, insofar as some intellectual ideas may be conveyed through a work of fine art, but that still requires promoting the epistemic role of reason at the expense of the senses. However, following suit, for Kant, knowledge is limited by the faculties of the mind, that is, by the fact of biology. Generally, however, this modernist, Cartesian legacy whereby reason and the passions are separated I have suggested, underpins thinking of the arts and ethics as subjective (or intersubjective), and physics as objective.

Naturalism has left its adherents of two minds about the arts. They are apt to accept aesthetic relativism, but they seek out the universal variables of aesthetic appreciation. In other words, they recognize that aesthetic appreciation is bound by solidarity, but they also think that our limits may be universal, taking us beyond the bounds of consensus. What has become apparent since the age of reason took hold is that merely uncovering the biological variables in understanding why we think a work of say, Raphael (1483–1520) or Rembrandt (1606–1669) is beautiful does little to help us understand if there is a rational basis for thinking so.

The problem of the naturalist's slide into subjectivism arises at least in part because of the separation of truth from beauty. On the first score, beauty is no longer considered an object, like an apple, but a property of one. Second, the property of being beautiful we have come to conceive as an act of projection founded in our inclinations (e.g., my desire for an apple). Taken together, we are left with the old cliché: beauty lies in the eye of the beholder.

HEGEL: IDEALISM OR RELATIVISM

The tension between idealism and realism is reflected in aesthetics because we can feel pulled in two directions: we acknowledge the cultural specificity of artworks; but also feel the universality of their beauty. Hegel is well known to have based his philosophical idealism on a reunification of these two polar opposites, the particular, where we embrace for instance, cultural pluralism; and the universal, or absolute truth.

Yet, the challenges involved in making Hegel's thought relevant to aesthetics today are daunting and are intimated by Bungay's claim in *Beauty and Truth: A Study of Hegel's Aesthetics*: "Nobody really knows what Hegel wanted to do."[23] Some commentators wish to understand Hegel's aesthetics in light of his metaphysics and others place the emphasis elsewhere.[24] If Hegel's metaphysics was central to understanding his aesthetics, there is on-going debate about interpreting him there.[25]

In fact, Bungay was concerned that Hegel's connection of beauty and truth "belongs on the scrap-heap of history."[26] Bungay also claimed, however, that by studying Hegel's writings on the fine arts "subtle solutions to

---

23. Bungay, *Beauty and Truth*, v. Also see Paolucci, *Hegel, On the Arts* (originally published as *Vorlesungen über die Ästhetik* in 1842–43).

24. Desmond, "Art and the Absolute"; Halper, "Logic of Art"; Wicks, "Hegel's Aesthetics."

25. Williamson, *Introduction to Hegel's Philosophy of Religion*, 1984.

26. Bungay, *Beauty and Truth*, 9.

modern problems emerge,"[27] and other scholars concur that his thought has contemporary relevance.[28]

The Hegelian approach can be considered a comprehensive one to the extent he sought to unify the concerns of rationalists and empiricists in a way that did not terminate in Kantian subjectivism. Orienting ourselves by Hegel's metaphysics, we can look to *The Encyclopaedia Logic*, where he clarifies the relationship between essences and appearances. Hegel wrote, "Essence therefore is not *behind* or *beyond* appearance, but since essence is what exists, existence is appearance."[29] He went on, "It [appearance] is the infinite goodness that releases its semblance into immediacy and grants it the joy of being-there . . . Appearance is precisely the truth of being."[30] To understand what all this means we can juxtapose Hegel's thought to Kant's.

Hegel agreed with Kant in this: the beauty of the fine arts is greater than that of nature because it is a "product of mind."[31] Contrary to Kant, however, Hegel held that in art the spiritual appears in sensuous shape. The goal of art, for Hegel, is to reveal the truth in sensuous form manifest in history as a way of knowing the absolute.

Thus, Hegel approached the arts by considering the times in which they were created: in the oldest arts we witness a spiritualization of nature; in the classical period, humans were the focus; and in the romantic period, artists probed an infinite subjectivity. Art, then, also has a historical role by making the past present. Hegel's account of tragedy is a useful illustration of his metaphysics. For him, great Greek Tragedies like the *Oedipus Rex* of Sophocles "raised our awareness to the necessity of things."[32] Poetry is a way to truth, for Hegel, because in it we see the idea of the unfolding of the absolute idea in particular lives and societies.

Art, for Hegel, aims at the identification between the eternal and temporal, whereby truth is "revealed in real appearance to our external perception."[33] As Hegel explained, with art we deal "with the liberation of the mind from the content and forms of the finite: with the presence and

---

27. Ibid.
28. Aitken, *Biological Origins of Art*; Etter, *Between Transcendence and Historicism*.
29. EL, § 131. With the *Encyclopaedia of Logic*, I cite the section of the book.
30. Ibid., § 131.
31. PFA, 2.
32. Ibid., 52.
33. Ibid., 199.

reconciliation of the absolute in the sensory and phenomenonal."[34] All the various stages of art, classical or romantic, for instance, are just various realization of the absolute idea.

Hegel's account of drama matches his overall metaphysics, whereby an all encompassing absolute idea contains all the moments of history.[35] Similarly, he claimed the highest dramas elaborate content and form as a whole, whose entire organization is aimed towards the "final end."[36] We witness, in a tragedy, a "collision of forces,"[37] including universal ones that are realized and merged in a particular character.

One way to make sense of the claim that art has a connection to truth goes like this: we think that art tells us something about the times in which we live. It is a window into the socio-cultural world in which we live. Bradley, an Oxonian poet and Shakespearian scholar, said in his *Oxford Lectures on Poetry* that the conflict between the laws of men and divine ones touch at the heart of Hegel's account.

We are stuck between two worlds, Hegel's talk of the absolute, on the one hand, and his attention to history, on the other. Yet if art expresses the central metaphysics of each civilization, each seems to understand the absolute imperfectly, at least until we reach the end of history.

Bungay emphasized, though art presents the absolute of each civilization, at the same time however, for Hegel art is "mixed up" the notion of a *Weltanshauungen* or worldview.[38] Hegel's relevance, at least to postmodern ears, is to sever off his metaphysics and pay attention to the notion of differing worldviews. We are led to wonder, nonetheless, if the cultural aspect that Hegel discussed only renders art more subjective than Kant had already done.

Whatever universality we can attribute to aesthetic judgement with Kant becomes splintered through the prism of history for Hegel. Further, we still need to explain why we should think that art is both historically contingent and a window into the universal truth, which harkens us back to Bradley's concern of what I called being caught between two worlds, our finite one and God's infinite one.

---

34. Ibid., 200.
35. Guyer, "Thought and Being"; Halper, "Logic of Art"; Wicks, "Hegel's Aesthetics."
36. Paolucci and Paolucci, *Hegel on Tragedy*, 63.
37. Ibid., 126.
38. Bungay, *Beauty and Truth*, 60.

Part III: Contrasts and Reflections

Pillow, in a study of both Kant's and Hegel's aesthetics claimed that for Kant art provides an "uncanny" moment that exhausts concepts, at best, an experience of "sublime indeterminacy."[39] Yet, as Pillow noted, Kant fell back on the dichotomy of the subject and the object, separating aesthetics from rational ideas. Hegel's thought, he also emphasized, culminated in reasons unification of thought and the world, namely art, religion, and philosophy.

There are traditionally at least two ways to bridge the chasm between ourselves and God, faith or mysticism. Desmond in *Art and the Absolute* explained that, for Hegel, art overcomes the distinction between "I" and "God" because the artist is a confluence of herself and history. As Desmond noted, for Plato, the object that is beauty, truth, and goodness were held together in a holy trinity, which transcend the temporal world.[40] Desmond had noted that we have been shipwrecked between thinking either that beauty is an intrinsic characteristic of an object, as Plato held, or the result of the mind's constructive powers, as Kant claimed. "Hegel's concrete universal," Desmond wrote, "need not be seen as a simple repudiation of the Platonic search for the universal, but rather as an attempt at its concrete completion."[41]

For Hegel, appearances, temporality, subjectivity, and practices are precisely the way through which we come to know God. Our particular practices are an expression of our most cherished ideas, and taken together in the sum of history, coextensive with the absolute one.

Etter in *Between Transcendence and Historicism: The Ethical Nature of the Arts in Hegel's Aesthetics* explained that Hegel's concept of the divine involves both "absoluteness and contingency."[42] Refining Pillows expression, Etter claimed that for Hegel, together art, religion, and philosophy are modes of knowing the absolute.

Looking at truth through Hegelian eyes is at odds with our modern outlook. Frege, in the beginning of his famous paper "Thoughts," claimed that the *good* concerns ethics, *beauty* concerns aesthetics, and *truth* concerns logic. In Frege's terms, beauty was all about discovery (e.g., feelings) without justification. In one form or another, the separation of beauty from truth has been canonical since at least the nineteenth century.[43] It is com-

---

39. Pillow, *Sublime Understanding*, 25, 136.
40. Desmond, *Art and the Absolute*.
41. Ibid., 127.
42. Etter, *Between Transcendence and Historicism*, 209.
43. Frege, *The Foundations of Arithmetic* (originally published as *Grundlagen der*

monplace to hold since at least Frege, the originator of the linguistic turn (i.e., the idea that an analysis of language is the way to clarify our ontology), that there is a difference between the contexts of discovery, a psychological matter, from the context of justification. That is, following Frege, we are led to think of art as inextricably a psychological affair.

Yet if we hold fast to Hegel's metaphysics, a number of things come to pass. To begin with, we must keep in mind, for Hegel, everything becomes a moment in the process that is the absolute idea. We can say with Hegel, then, that art is an expression of truth insofar as it a reflection of our story; in turn, our story is part of a historical one; and it is part of the unfolding of the absolute. For Hegel, art can provide us both the absolute truths of our civilization and those that are transcendent, for the appropriate audience. According to Hegel, fine art lets us glimpse the truth, writ small and large.

HEGEL'S LEGACY

Hegel's fusion of essence and appearance brings with it the revaluation of the role of subjectivity. No longer are the senses merely defective instruments that need to be mastered by reason and limited by its reach. Rather, works of fine art, so-called, accomplish the aim of the speculative philosopher—reflecting the mind back upon itself, that is, ideally, upon the absolute sensuous idea. In other words, through art we express the paradoxical nature of the world, for Hegel, which is spiritual, being constructed by a mind, yet having a physical form.

The following summary is helpful to connect to Heidegger's thought:

1. As a consequence of a rupture in our relationship to Being, proponents of the early Cartesian approaches incline us to think that aesthetic appreciation relative.
2. Kant placed art within the intersubjective realm.
3. For Hegel, art can be a vehicle to truth.
4. For both Hegel and Heidegger, we are caught up in the unfolding of history.

In art, our experiences are raised to the level of moments of the absolute. Recall, Hegel's strategy is to conceive of particulars and universals as

---

Arithmetik in 1884). Also Frege, "Thoughts" (originally published as *Beiträgenzun und Philosophie des Deutschen I* in 1918–19).

illuminating each other. A particular work of art reflects its historical time, but in allowing us to generalize about place, it is also an expression of the absolute.

For Hegel, to speak of beauty entails a discussion of truth, history, and the reconciliation between the particular with the absolute. For him, radical idealism is the most robust realism because it includes everything, even beauty. So with a Hegelian aesthetics, we can have our idealism and realism.

In sum, Hegel's aesthetics in light of his logic, allowing us insight into Heidegger's own German, idealist tendencies. The unfolding of Hegel's absolute idea is transformed in Heidegger's writings as the destiny of Being.

The consequences for a Heideggerian ethic goes like this. With Heidegger, since he focuses his attention on our loss of relationship with Being, we can at least infer that he is taken by a closer connection between truth, beauty, and Being than modern thinkers would allow. Heidegger prompts us to call into question the separation of metaphysics from the arts and ethics.

We can understand why Heidegger thought that ethics requires a fundamental relationship to Being. Namely, with that primordial relationship, we are put in a state of mind where we have ethical sentiments. The fact we can empathize with other entails we see some commonality between us, even if it is just being sensuous. If the passions, properly cultivated, bind us together in an ethical fellowship, experienced as a moral harmony akin to the beauty we feel when witnessing the harmonizing starry skies, some such sublime feeling may very well be the foundation of a Heideggerian ethics.

9

Schweitzer's Ethics

My purpose in this chapter is to utilize Schweitzer's mysticism, who was a philosopher and medical doctor, to illustrate a possible shape a Heideggerian ethic can take. Schweitzer said, "Reverence for life means to be in the grasp of the infinite, inexplicable, forward urging Will in which all Being is grounded."[1] In making my case, I shall draw heavily upon his *Out of My Life and Thought: An Autobiography*.

I first elucidate Schweitzer's ethics. I shall argue, second, that his notion of reverence for life can be seen as an example of what Heidegger is aiming at in the claim that we should engage in "letting beings be." Finally, I consider the implications for "letting beings be philosophy" in two disparate cases: (1) animal rights, and (2), the public-private distinction. In elucidating a Heideggerian ethic by allusions to Schweitzer, I do not intend to defend Schweitzer's thought.

SCHWEITZER'S CRITIQUE

Schweitzer had misgivings about the idea common to the enlightenment that civilization was progressing.[2] In fact, he went as far as to contend that material progress makes civilization more difficult.[3] He defined civilization as a mental disposition—namely, an ethical one—of the member

---

1. *PC*, 283.
2. Schweitzer, *Out of My Life*, 146.
3. *PC*, 87.

individuals.[4] An ethical attitude, he contends, consists in an "affirmation of the world and of life."[5] The inability to defend an ethical view of life, according to him, is a sign of the decay of civilization.

He opens part 2 of *The Philosophy of Civilization*: "My subject is the tragedy of the western world-view."[6] He wrote, "I recognized that the catastrophe of civilization stemmed from a catastrophe of attitude. The ideals of true civilization had become powerless because the idealistic attitude towards life in which they are rooted had gradually been lost to us. All events that occur within nations and within mankind can be traced to spiritual causes contained in the prevailing attitude towards life."[7]

Schweitzer is critical of a notion of progress that is bereft of an ethical ideal.[8] He claims, "Without such a general spiritual experience there is no possibility of holding our world back from the ruin and disintegration towards which it is being hastened."[9] Characterizing his time as lacking reason, he wrote, "We are living today under the sin of the collapse of civilization."[10]

He thinks that the pedantic character of modern philosophy is symptomatic of the decline of western civilization.[11] He wrote, "All that I had learned from philosophy about ethics left me in the lurch. The conceptions of the Good which it had offered were all so lifeless, so unelemental, so narrow, and so destitute of content that it was quite impossible to bring them into union with the affirmative attitude."[12]

His solution to the lack of foundation for ethics came while on a river in Africa, in the idea of reverence for life. As he recalls, "The iron door had yielded: The path in the thicket had become visible. Now I had found my way to the idea in which affirmation of the world and ethics are contained side by side!"[13]

---

4. Ibid., xii–xiii, 51.
5. *AU*, 150.
6. *PC*, 71.
7. *AU*, 149.
8. Ibid.
9. *PC*, xv.
10. Ibid., 37, 1.
11. Ibid., 6.
12. *AU*, 155.
13. Ibid., 156.

His principle of reverence for life: "I am life which wills to live, in the midst of life which wills to live."[14] He wrote, "I can do nothing but hold to the fact that the will-to-live in me manifests itself as will-to-live which desires to become one with other will-to-live."[15]

He contends that if religion affirms life that leads to civilization, otherwise decay sits on the horizon.[16] For Schweitzer, the decay or religion is part of the decline of civilization: "Two perceptions cast their shadow over my existence. One consists in my realization that the world is inexplicably mysterious and full of suffering; the other in the fact that I have been born into a period of spiritual decadence."[17] He emphasized the will, yet sees the only way of finding meaning in existence is by rising above the brute will to live, insofar as we are to show reverence for life.[18]

He put all his faith in rational thinking.[19] He tells us, "Renunciation of thinking is a declaration of spiritual bankruptcy."[20] Yet at the same time, he wrote, "The ethics, then, which originates in thinking is not 'according to reason,' but non-rational and enthusiastic."[21] That is to say, the basis of ethics lies not within the bounds of reason as Kant thought, but an experience, much like the one Schweitzer had on a river in Africa. He criticized Kant, writing, "Only such a thinking as establishes the sway of the mental attitude of reverence for life can bring mankind into perpetual peace."[22]

Schweitzer's explains, "I felt, too, that the fundamental thought of Stoicism true, namely that man must bring him into a spiritual relationship with the world and become one with it. In its essence, Stoicism is a nature philosophy that ends up in mysticism."[23] In fact, he also noted how the Stoics and Lao-Tzu have a similar philosophy, emphasizing resignation and inactivity, respectively.[24] He even praised Lord Shaftsbury for a "living philosophy of nature in collaboration with ethics."[25]

14. Ibid., 157.
15. *PC*, 312.
16. *AU*, 182.
17. Ibid., 219.
18. Ibid., 220.
19. Ibid., 222.
20. Ibid.
21. Ibid., 234.
22. *PC*, 334.
23. *AU*, 225.
24. Ibid., 225–26.
25. *PC*, 164.

Schweitzer is sceptical, however, about what mysticism can offer the ethicist: "Of all mysticism of the past it must be said that its ethical content is too slight. It puts men on the road of inwardness but not a living ethic."[26] Mysticism he complained, requires little ethical consequences, and often, for instance on his readings of Indian philosophers, a negative view of life.[27] "Mysticism is not the friend of ethics but its foe . . . And yet the ethic which is to satisfy thought must be born of mysticism."[28] He went on, "It [the question concerning the meaning of life] can be really answered only by a philosophy which brings man into a spiritual inward relation to Beings from which there result a natural necessity ethics both passive and active."[29]

Ethics, for Schweitzer, must originate in mysticism.[30] His mysticism is "the living devotion to Being which lives."[31] We aim, according to him, to become one with the infinite will, which he said is the same as love.[32] Life is sacred, according to him, if we accept the principle of reverence for life.[33] "The ethic of Reverence for Life is the ethic of Love widened to universality. It is the ethic of Jesus, now recognized as a consequent of his thought."[34] He pictured the ethical ideal thus: "He injures and destroys life only under necessity which he cannot avoid, and never from thoughtlessness. So far as he is a free man he uses every opportunity of taking the blessedness of being able to assist life and avert from it suffering and destruction."[35] He explains, "The view of Reverence for life is ethical mysticism. It allows union with the infinite to be realized by ethical action."[36]

He thinks that the church undermined authentic spirituality. He seeks, rather, an experience of God as "will-to-love."[37] The metaphysical and ethical overlap in his explanation: "They [many shoots] all come from a common root that existed at the start. That is, how the deeds of kind-

---

26. *AU*, 228.
27. *PC*, 302.
28. Ibid., 303.
29. Ibid.
30. Ibid., 304.
31. Ibid., 306.
32. Ibid., 341.
33. Ibid., 310.
34. *AU*, 232.
35. Ibid., 234.
36. Ibid., 235.
37. Ibid., 237, 238.

ness should be spread . . . Learn to see it [gratitude] as a mysterious law of existence. In obedience to it we have to fulfil our destiny."[38] Broadly, he thinks society can express ethical principles in law, but rests the basis of ethics in the individual struggle for the truth.[39] In fact, he contends that the collapse of civilization is consequent to leaving ethics to society.[40] To be civilized, he said, is to remain human, despite the conditions of modern civilization.[41] Reverence for life has a religious character.[42]

He tells us, "Surrendering himself to the guidance of this mysticism, man finds, meaning for his life in that he strove to accomplish his own spiritual and ethical self-fulfilment."[43] He contended, "All profound worldview is mysticism . . . spiritual self-devotion to the mysterious infinite Will which is continuously manifest in the universe."[44]

Though he, further, claims there can be no science of ethics, we can turn to experience: "All that one can do is to impart to him so much as one finds in oneself of that which ought to influence everybody, though better thought out perhaps, and stranger and clearer, so that the noise has become a musical note."[45]

REVERENCE FOR LIFE

Martin, who has written on the concept of reverence of life, attempts to revive it without the metaphysical luggage that has been unpopular in the later half of the twentieth century. Martin notes, however, "Schweitzer's metaphysics has some interest. It shares a kinship with the worldviews of Spinoza, Hinduism, Buddhism, and Native American religions."[46] Martin also noted that though Schweitzer was critical of pantheism (often associated with Indian philosophies), as a basis for an ethics, "he is not as metaphysically sceptical as he claims."[47] For Schweitzer, God and life are the

38. *RL,* 141.
39. *PC,* 327.
40. Ibid., 328.
41. Ibid., 334.
42. *AU,* 236.
43. *PC,* xv.
44. Ibid., 79.
45. Ibid., 102, 103.
46. Martin, "Rethinking Reverence," 168.
47. Ibid., 169.

same thing (pantheism) or, at the very least, the former pervades the later (panentheism); he is committed to some form of mysticism, which it is not my purpose to adjudicate between. Suffice it to say, he does rest ethics on a metaphysical basis, requiring cognitive access to via a mystical experience.

Baram, in a detailed essay, "Schweitzer, Jainism, and Reverence for Life," attempts to draw out the Indian sources for Schweitzer's thought, which goes to the heart of his mysticism. Baram wrote, "Ethical mysticism implies an active relationship between the human person and other life; through interaction with other life, union with the Divine is afforded."[48] Baram denies, however, that Schweitzer is a pantheist.[49] Baram explains, "He [Schweitzer] departs from mysticism as traditionally understood; it is mysticism not only to a heightened spiritual end but also to a higher ethical purpose."[50]

It has been thought problematic to derive an ethics from mysticism; we do not exist as separate entities if mysticism-cum-pantheism is correct. It is the life denying aspects of some Indian philosophies—the world is an illusion etc.—that Schweitzer is wary about.[51] Since the world contains a great deal of killing, why does not bonding with the universal will-to-live lead to fascism?[52] A mystical union with the universal will-to-live may not entail ethical consequences.

In Jainism, according to Baram, Schweitzer finds a companion, which points the way. Baram remarks, "Schweitzer and Jainism affirm the inherent or intrinsic value in all life. Both believe that all life-forms have value in-themselves, independent of human estimations; all living things are to be protected and reverenced as far as possible."[53] By making a connection to Jainism, Baram, once again, makes it safe to view Schweitzer as a mystic. Schweitzer's mysticism results in an acknowledgement of the intrinsic value of all life. Indian mysticism, nevertheless, sets the tone for his own, regardless of how simplistic his reading of it is.

In Christianity, in addition to the notions of God and love, there is a social program. Consider several passages:

---

48. Barsam, "Schweitzer, Jainism," 216.
49. Ibid., 217.
50. Ibid., 218.
51. Ibid., 226.
52. Ibid., 220.
53. Ibid., 239.

Schweitzer's Ethics

> Blessed are you who are poor, for yours is the Kingdom of God.[54]
> [God] who executes justice for the oppressed.[55]
> He gathers the outcastes of Israel. He heals the broken-hearted, and binds up their wounds. He counts the number stars and gives names to all of them.[56]

Nothing is too small to be of concern to God:

> But the very hairs of your head are all numbered.[57]

The concern for the oppressed is obvious in Schweitzer's concern for the rights of animals. He speaks for those that do not have a voice. Another of the sources for Schweitzer is the Bible.

He fused the pantheism of Indian thought with the concern for the oppressed typical of Christianity; the result is an ethical mysticism, on the one hand, and the pantheism of Christ, on the other. He avoided, respectively, life-denial (which he associates with Indian thought, and the lack of ethical foundations (which he perhaps worries about as a Christian theologian). By combining the two, he can emphasize, the positive ethical consequences of Indian mysticism (*ahimsa* or reverence for life), and the mystical element in Christianity—the scholastic notion that creation emanates from God. By drawing on Indian and Christian sources his thought is unique.

At the same time, many commentators have remarked upon Schweitzer's ambiguity towards mysticism.[58] Several famous passages are usually cited from Schweitzer's famous two-volume magnum opus, *The Philosophy of Civilization*, where he denies ethics can be found on mysticism.[59]

So far, in this chapter, I have been attempting to establish that Schweitzer is committed to mysticism and that it serves as the foundation for an ethics of reverence for life. Yet, my aim is to show how reverence for life can help us elucidate a Heideggerian ethic.

There are connections between Schweitzer and Heidegger. First, Schweitzer and Heidegger see the world in a state of decay. For Schweitzer, we have the wrong attitude towards the world. Schweitzer and Heidegger do not separate the withdrawal of being from material advancement. The

---

54. Luke 6:20.
55. Ps 146:7.
56. Ps 147:2–4.
57. Matt 10:30.
58. Barsam, "Schweitzer, Jainism."
59. *PC*, 302–3.

scepticism with which Schweitzer views technological progress resonates with Heidegger. As Heidegger would say, we force nature to conform to our aims. Our ends, moreover, contain a limited respect for the natural world. We are misrelated to nature, which is a symptom of a metaphysical malady, in Heideggerian terms, the withdrawal of being.

Second, for both thinkers, we have to have a pantheistic experience of nature to set things right. For Schweitzer, there is a desire for a mystical experience, where God is experienced in the diversity of creation. Heidegger aims at establishing a fundamental relationship to being. Since Heidegger seeks to avoid Platonism, it is plausible to think that he also must find a relationship to being within the world. That is to say, a fundamental relationship to being must be mediated, as it were, through beings.

Third, and in fact, both look to the past to find examples of when we had the correct attitude towards the world. The correct attitude is to be found in thinkers with a robust metaphysics. The paradigms are the Stoics, Lao-Tzu, Indian philosophies, for Schweitzer, and the Pre-Socratics for Heidegger. Schweitzer seeks a fundamental relationship to being through beings; much the same can be said, as I have already indicated, for Heidegger. Their sources are telling.

Fourth, ethics, for Schweitzer and Heidegger, finds its motivation in a mystical experience. The experience of the sublime entails that we submit ourselves to the effects of an experience of nature. Here, it is hard not to think of Thoreau (discussed further in the ensuing section, "Environmentalism"). The mystical experience discussed, by Schweitzer, entails, also, submissive consequences: Having a sense of security that things are unfolding as they should, that truth is stronger than circumstance (in the end), and that—against protestations, on occasion—it is the best of all possible worlds. That is to say, according to Schweitzer and Heidegger, we should accept the world. The word "submission" suggests extreme pacifism; yet, it need not. I shall have more to say about the notions of acceptance and submission in this section.

Finally, where Schweitzer's ethics terminates in reverence for life, Heidegger's in letting beings be. I have attempted to show that there is, in both cases, an attempt to found an ethics on an attitude. Letting beings be is reverence for life.

Schweitzer worried about the ethical consequences of Indian philosophies because they were life-rejecting, and too, passive; Heidegger's notion of letting beings be, also is perhaps so. Are to let things take their course? After all, history is part, according to Heidegger, of the destiny of being.

Letting beings be is negative, in that it requires that we do not do something. Yet, letting beings be, can also be active. We would be letting beings be, if knowing something's nature, we helped it. In fact, we have to interpret "letting beings be" to allow some disturbance of nature, as both Schweitzer and the Jains, for example, in their own ways, realized; it is not possible to live without some disturbance—and killing. The ethical point, however, is to adopt the attitude, of letting beings be, that expresses reverence for life. Letting beings be thus motivates action.

Schweitzer was born January 14, 1857, in Kaysersberg in Upper Alsace, a German area that became French. He represents a romantic grain of thought, critical of technological progress, and defends metaphysics. His writings are punctuated by mixed messages about the enlightenment project. He also accepts a metaphysical and non-rational basis for ethics. If Heidegger's ethics is to follow Schweitzer, there are two possible consequences for our view of the environment and professionalism, which I shall explore next. These cases are tentative and only intended to provide examples of what implications a Heideggerian mystical ethics, drawn along the lines of Schweitzer, might have. Given the terse lines about Heidegger has left us, however, such an exploration, I think, is altogether welcome.

ENVIRONMENTALISM

Thoureau, an American environmental mystic, is where I begin the story of environmentalism I shall tell. Thoreau wrote of his heuristic: "Neither method nor discipline can supersede the necessity of being forever on the alert. What is a course of history, or philosophy, or poetry, no how well selected, or the best society, or the most admirable routine of life, compared with the discipline of looking always at what is seen? Will you be a reader, a student merely, or a seer?"[60] He reported:

> I went to the woods because I wished to live deliberately, to confront only the essential facts of life, and see if I could learn what it had to teach, and not, when I came to die, discover that I had not lived . . . I wanted to live deep and suck out the marrow of life, to live sturdily and Spartan like as to rout all that was not life . . . if it was mean, why then to get the whole genuine meanness of it, and

60. Thoreau, *Walden*, 157.

> publish its meanness to the world; or if it were sublime, to know by experience, and be able to give a true account of it . . .[61]

He went on, "Be it life or death, we crave only reality. If we are really dying, let us hear the rattle in our throats and feel the cold in the extremities . . ."[62]

Putting differences aside, we can observe the following salient points of contact with Schweitzer, Thoreau, and Heidegger. For Schweitzer, Heidegger and Thoreau, we obtain a fundamental relationship with being/nature, which becomes the basis of an ethical orientation towards the world. Thoreau's reverence for nature did result in letting beings be. He practiced what Heidegger preached.

So far, I suggested Heidegger's philosophy is at least consistent with an environmental philosophy, which reveres all life. Sometimes environmentalists, like Paul Watson, a founding member of Greenpeace, however, attempt to define themselves against an interpretation of Judeo-Christian thought, drawn from Genesis.

> Then God said, "Let Us make man in Our image; according to Our likeness; let them have dominion over the fish of the sea, over the birds of the air, and over the cattle, over all the earth and over every creeping thing that creeps on the earth." So God created man in the image of God He created him; male and female He created them. The God blessed them, and God said to them, "Be fruitful and multiply; fill the earth and subdue it; have dominion over the fish of the sea, over the birds of the air, and over every living thing that moves on earth."[63]

According to Watson, Judeo-Christian thought entails (1) separation all of creation from humans; (2) places humans above the rest of creation, and finally, (3), legitimates the notion that everything is here for us. Admittedly, for the Heidegger of 1927, we can see some commonality in the special status he gave to Dasein, putting him at odds with Schweitzer. Yet, emphasizing Heidegger's later works, the centrality of Dasein is displaced in favor of being.

I suggested, in chapter 6, the idea of intrinsic value is Heideggerian, a consequence of the philosophy of being. Environmentalists, and animal rights activists, who I shall use for the purpose of illustration, often emphasize (a) the commonality of all life, (b), its ecology, and (c), the notion

61. Ibid., 135.
62. Ibid., 142.
63. Gen 1:26–28.

Schweitzer's Ethics

that nature has intrinsic value (therefore, above and beyond nature's human utility). There are differences between environmentalists and animal rights activists, but they share commonalities alluded to, which bring them into the fold of Schweitzer, suffice it to say.

Let us take a look to the contextual differences between Schweitzer and the modern animal rights movement. The time of the Old Testament was that of an agrarian society, which pre-dating the birth of Christ, was over at least two thousand years old. It would have been a time where "subduing" nature would have been necessary for survival in an immediate way. Commerce with animals would have been common. We had an intimate and domineering connection to the land. The passages from Genesis that Watson took offence to are descriptive, however. That is, it is plausible to think that the passages from Genesis reflect an entire world, which is articulated as prescriptions.

Jumping ahead to the late twentieth century, when modern animal rights philosophy came on the scene, we find an industrialized world. It is the historically extreme treatment of animals that we find in modernity, I think, that motivated the animal rights movement.

Entities have rights according to Singer, often cited as the well spring of the modern animal rights movement, because of their ability of feel pleasure and pain. Taken together—the extreme abuse of animals and the secularization of thought—provided the basis for of the animal rights movement.

What I have suggested so far is that two competing ways of orienting ourselves towards nature, the anthropocentric and environmentalist, are philosophies that grew out of and reflect two very different ways of life. Of course, pointing out the historical underpinnings of an ideology does not speak to its rightness or wrongness, as Schweitzer would bring to our attention.

I think that the animal rights activists must concede, however, that at certain time the use of animals for human purposes was a necessity, for example, when we were hunters and gathers. By the same cord, we must also concede, however, that other things like cannibalism and human infanticide, which we today find morally repugnant, may have also been necessary for human survival.

As conditions improved, so the story goes, we were able to revise our ethics. For the moral realist, becoming ethical is a possibility that emerges for members of a society with the progress of human civilization.

Environmentalism, on the Heideggerian account, marks, I propose, the beginning of the fulfillment of an ethical eschatology.

BEING PROFESSIONAL

In addition to environmentalism, another feature of the modern world is professionalism, which entails the idea of the public-private split, whereby the two domains must be separated. Professionalism concerns only the public domain. I will scrutinize the public-private split from a Heideggerian point of view. I shall argue that professionalism must be mitigated to achieve excellent results that are also ethical. I begin with some personal reflections I had as a pre-service teacher in junior-senior kindergarten and a business experience that illustrates the tension between public policy and personal experiences in the field. Due to the personal nature of the observations, we should not to take observations out of context.

My experience as a student, was guided by the ideal of professionalism. Much of our student lives, especially as master and doctorial candidates, is with our teachers. When I was a doctoral student at the University of Ottawa, professors were discouraged from going out with students for a drink, which seemed quite common in the previous generation of scholars.

When a Bachelor's of Education student, my first teaching placement was in junior-senior kindergarten, an adjustment having passed my PhD thesis several years earlier. I had, also, no experience with children and had no idea if I would like them. When I was a student at in the Bachelor's of Education Program at the University of Windsor, I was told, "The rule is we do not touch children." Also, the children "are not our friends." From afar, it is a reasonable assertion.

Children of this age are tactile creatures. They learn by painting, manipulation blocks, and can find pleasure in simple activities like jumping up and down to a song. Sometimes the kids would be in the hallway, on their way to the gymnasium, and a child would be, lost in her own world, hopping up and down. I would smile, pat her on the head and say, "Eyes up front."

In my first placement in Grade 1, a girl came up and hugged me; at the time, I was not exactly sure what was happening. I observed the associate teacher, in a kindergarten class, play with the children, chasing them, and picking them up as a father would, which would result in screams of joy from the class.

It is not that there is no ethical relationship between both parties. The point of these narratives is not to plea from more human contact between children or students. The world being what it is, there are obvious dangers for teachers if they do not strictly abide by professional standards.

Teachers do a job, which requires competence, reliability, efficiency, and creating interest in activities. The relationship between student and teacher is an economic one, in part. Teachers are hired, and students (their parents) are clients. At the heart of all professional-client relationships, is the ideal that it is not personal. At best, any transference is a natural error, which consists in thinking that the person you have hired is your friend.

For Aristotle, however, ethics was personal; it was about developing a certain character, which was expressed in all human relationships. Human relations, in fact, existed in a symbiotic relationship with the ethical person. The good life was a result of being ethical, and, there were prerequisites (food, friends, and so on).

According to Kant, however, ethics was about our relations with others, not our self. At the precipice of the self-other dichotomy was the private-public distinction. Private acts were of no moral consequence; public ones were. The idea of professionalism is rooted in an ideological event in Western history.

The complaints of romantics, like Heidegger, with modernity, loss of contact with nature, others, and loss of sense of self, are reflected in professionalism. Belonging to a profession is, of course, different than a family. We have colleagues, associates, and so on, and linguistically the terms cannot be considered semantically coextensive with friends. To the extent that we rigorously seek to be professional, we take the public-private split which occurred in the eighteenth century to its logical end, and whose horrors are represented in literary works like Kafka's *The Castle*.

In this chapter, I have argued that Schweitzer provides one way, with his notion of reverence for life, to reply to the criticism, that letting beings be is hopelessly vacuous and vague. Using Schweitzer's ethics to provide an illustration of a Heideggerian one, I drew out two implications, for environmentalists and professionalism. A Heideggerian ethic could buttress environmentalism along the lines of Schweitzer. Also, it can cause us to at least question the way we have separated the public from the private domain. In the next chapter, I focus upon how Heidegger's critique of onto-theology bears upon the problem of relativism.

10

A Heideggerian Rebuttal of Ethical Relativism

Heidegger offers no argument against ethical relativism, and hints at a time before philosophical disputations altogether. For Heidegger the problem of ethical relativism is a consequence of placing us in a false dilemma: either values are subjective and self-dependent or objective and mind-independent. I shall argue, rather, that values can be objective without assuming an inflated ontology.

First, I scrutinize two arguments in favor of ethical relativism, and suggest a pragmatist rebuttal. Second, I shall explain how Heidegger's ethical eschatology evades ethical relativism.

ETHICAL RELATIVISM'S TWO PILLARS

Ethical relativism has been buoyed up by two arguments. The first argument is negative: mind-independent values, like the good, do not exist. Second, the inductive argument: if our ethics have always changed, they always will. There is no human nature, as Maslow claimed. In the twentieth century, each argument has been propounded by a host of supporters.

Also, the two arguments for ethical relativism work in tandem. Since there are no mind-independent values (the negative argument), explains why ethical knowledge is always changing (the inductive argument). The reason there is no way to adjudicate between ethical systems is precisely because there is no mind-independent values to refer to. The negative argument has been taken up by philosophers who thought they were demystifying language, and is so doing, purging us of metaphysical disputes. Moore deemed the idea that the properties of an object could have intrinsic value as the naturalistic fallacy.[1] He claimed that the question "what is real" has no bearing on "what is good."[2] There seems to be a linguistic difference between facts (e.g., the pot weighs X) and values (it is a good pot). It would seem that the property of weight has an objectivity than evaluation lacks. J. L. Mackie, in fact, concludes in his influential study, *Ethics: Inventing Right and Wrong*, that objective values are shared values.[3]

Since there was no obvious reason to believe in mind-independent values, they must be, as the arch-positivist Ayer put it, psychological or sociological judgments.[4] Ayer tells us that ethical concepts are pseudo-concepts. According to him, the statement "you stole money" may have a truth value, but the contention "you stole money is wrong" does not.[5] Ethical words, he tells us, are meant to evoke a particular response.[6] Value disputes terminate in exchanges of verbal abuse; there can be no science of ethics.[7]

Emotivists were essentially Wittgenstien-inspired positivists, who held that philosophical problems resulted from linguistic confusion. For example, Stevenson, in *Ethics and Language*, thought that we get confused when we treat words like "good" as matters of fact. He held that we must distinguish disagreements of *belief* from those of *attitudes*.[8] According to him, scientific disputes are disagreements about beliefs, and ethical ones are conflicting attitudes.[9] "Good," he tells us, means "I approve of X and you should as well."[10] The point of moral language is to influence attitudes, and even when emotive words are used in science, they obscure the detachment necessary to get at the facts, he tells us.[11]

1. Moore, *Principia Ethica*, 10 (original work published in 1903).
2. Ibid., 113.
3. Mackie, *Cement of the Universe*, 235.
4. Ayer, "Critique of Ethics and Theology," 28.
5. Ibid., 30–31.
6. Ibid., 31.
7. Ibid., 33–34.
8. Stevenson, *Ethics and Language*, 1.
9. Ibid., 13.
10. Ibid., 21.
11. Ibid., 117, 243, 248, 336.

Similarly, Urmson, in *The Emotive Theory of Ethics*, explains that moral language is prescriptive.[12] He holds that the claim "X is good" can be true according to a standard for a certain type of things. For instance, we could say that "X is a good hammer." There remains, however, a difference between cases where something is considered a property (natural or otherwise) of things and a convention.

Sumner provides an example of the inductive argument, writing an influential book in the early twentieth century that documented the changing customs of humanity. His book has been influential, philosophically, because it has rendered obvious the notion that ethical relativism must be true.

Sumner uses the terms "folkways" to sum up the patterns of behavior of a group. He thinks that an inquiry into folkways may be considered as the study of society.[13] At the very basis of human existence he sees acts and needs.[14] According to him, there is very little that is innate, except the avoidance of pain.[15] As he puts it, folkways are produced by the repetition of petty acts.[16] They are amended when the cause pain.[17] Behaviors help us avoid pain become customs.

Ethics, according to him, is a "generalization from the experience of pleasure and pain which is won in efforts to carry on the struggle for existence under actual life conditions."[18] He concludes, "Morals is an impossible and unreal category. It has no existence [as an autonomous domain], and can have none."[19]

From the production of folkways come mores, institutions, and laws. We may think it important to dress a certain way, which may have just kept us from the cold. Over time, so the saying goes, patterns of dress become solidified as manners, customs, mores, morals, and finally, law.

Sumner said, "In folkways, what is, is right."[20] According to him, "Everything in the mores of a time and place must be regarded as justified with

12. Urmson, *Emotive Theory*, 37.
13. Sumner, *Folkways*, 34.
14. Ibid., 2.
15. Ibid.
16. Ibid., 3.
17. Ibid., 5.
18. Ibid., 29.
19. Ibid., 37.
20. Ibid., 28.

A Heideggerian Rebuttal of Ethical Relativism

regard to that time and place."[21] Furthermore, he holds that "there are no ethical forces in history."[22] We may wish to note that he thinks that fashion even in logic and mathematics change.[23] At any rate, taken together—the fact of ethical change and the rejection of a *telos* of history, leads to ethical relativism: "Therefore might has made all the right which ever has existed or exists now."[24] Interestingly, however, the very last passage of Sumner's conclusion flies in the face of his key idea: "If all try the policy of dishonesty, the result will be the firmest conviction that honesty is the best policy. The mores aim always to arrive at the correct notions of virtue. In so far as they reach the correct results the virtue policy proves to be the only success policy."[25]

Sumner hints that the success policy—acting to avoid pain—may not after all be at odds with the virtue policy. To believe that what is pragmatic and right may, in the end, cohere, seems to require the assumption of metaphysics of history which he has already denied. Nevertheless, suffice it to say, to take seriously that mores aim at "the correct notions of virtue" requires that ethical standards must be more than the caprice of a time and place, or an incredibly lucky accident. There are reasons to consider the idea that history may have a moral end. I shall have more to say about a moral eschatology in § "Abraham Maslow."

Gadamer, a student of Heidegger, provides an example of the postmodern strategy. He advocated the idea of "the hermeneutic circle," that is, human understanding is facilitated by pre-understandings. Ethical practices are contingent upon prejudices germane to a historical time period. Foucault, another Heidegger-inspired writer, conducts an archaeology of knowledge, in order to trace the manifestation of different regimes power/knowledge in the prison, asylum, medical establishment, and other institutions. In both cases, metaphysics is replaced by sociology and history. All knowledge, including ethics, is relative.

More recently, the idealist strain of Heidegger's thought has also been taken up by Rorty, a contemporary American pragmatist. He offers an interesting contemporary case for ethical relativism; he takes seriously both the negative and positive argument, as well as speaking to our unease with

21. Ibid., 58.
22. Ibid., 476.
23. Ibid., 193.
24. Ibid., 66.
25. Ibid., 653.

Part III: Contrasts and Reflections

ethical relativism. According to Rorty, the notion that we can prove that a set of claims is "true" in such a way that make appeal to the real world is bankrupt; there are, for him, no mind-independent values.[26] According to Rorty, furthermore, appealing to one's intuitions, say common sense, is naive because it is blind to contingencies.[27] He doubts that there are ethical fundamentals, which are invariant in all cultures and for all times.

Rorty divides philosophers into those that are ironic and those who are not.[28] According to him, an ironic philosopher believes, for instance, that X is good, but concedes there is no metaphysical reason to think so. The ironist, for her part, recognizes contingency, yet maintains belief in X as useful. Foucault and Gadamer, contemporary moral relativists, emphasize the idealist strain in Heidegger's thought, that is, the notion of historical change without eschatology. Postmodernists share, with the positivists, a rebuke of metaphysics. Instead of defending the metaphysical basis of ethics, they further demote that of science. They blur the distinction between science and other human institutions. The postmodern approach to ethics, consequently, would embrace the gist of Sumner's book.

We can wonder about the subjectivity or objectivity of values, which are implicit in our judgements.[29] Subjectivism entails the conclusion that there is nothing that is right or wrong.[30] As Sayre-McCord remarks, "Indeed, for the greater part of this century the dominant view in philosophy has been that these [moral realist] convictions cannot be justified."[31]

In this book, it has not been my purpose to argue against ethical relativism, which has already been done. Rather, my aim has been to develop an alternative, Heideggerian account of ethics that is realist. To make the Heideggerian account plausible, however, the arguments in favor of ethical relativism must be shown to allow of a reply, which I explain as follows.

Upon the eschatological view, history is moving in a direction that will bring about circumstances that give rise to an ethics. Sumner, ironically, comes close to an eschatological ethics.

There has been various attempts to defend the universality of ethical judgements, like McDowell's interesting argument that values are secondary

---

26. Rorty, *Contingency*, 5.
27. Ibid., 74.
28. Ibid., xiii, xv, 5.
29. Hooker, *Truth in Ethics*.
30. Ibid.
31. Sayre-McCord, *Essays on Moral Realism*, ix.

A Heideggerian Rebuttal of Ethical Relativism

qualities.[32] Basically the idea is that there are mind-independent primary qualities (e.g., sound waves) that when confronted by a subject give rise to secondary qualities (e.g., we hear beautiful music). If we all have the same reactions to an object—say we all think sugar sweet, for instance—we may be able to maintain the universality of ethical judgements by contending that values are secondary qualities: normal responses to a certain stimuli. To adopt the words of the moral realist, Boyd, taken from a different context, to ask "why X is good" is to suffer a cognitive defect.[33]

The idea of being an ethical realist and denying, for instance, the mind-independence of values may be counterintuitive for the positivism typical of the twentieth century to being with. It is worth noting that moral realism without an expanded ontology, however, is not without precedent. For Aquinas, for instance, the first principles of natural law were not inferred from nature, speculative principles, facts, or about nature of good and evil, or a teleological concept of nature (or any other concept of nature).[34] As Aquinas put it, "The good of the human being is to be in accord with reason and human evil is being outside the order of reasonableness."[35] Taken as self-evident, are basic values (e.g., life, friendship, play, knowledge, aesthetic experience, practical reasonableness, religion) that underlie human conduct.[36] Understanding what is practical requires knowledge of human wants and the human condition.[37] The end result is that both what we are, and the conditions in which we find ourselves prod us towards morality. For example, mutual trustworthiness is the basis for common life, which is necessary on an individual and social level.[38] Going back to Aristotle, ethics rested on obtaining the ideal type of a person.

These attempts tally with commentators that seek a Heideggerian ethics in his analysis of Dasein, so leave them aside. But Heidegger's strategy that we have being pursuing—of putting the being-question at the forefront—is even further foreign than seeking ethical realism without ontologically reifying values. Also, the nature of Dasein is not completely

---

32. McDowell, "Values and Secondary Qualities," 175, 178, 180.
33. Boyd, "Materialism without Reductionism," 215.
34. Finnis, *Natural Law*, 33.
35. As cited in ibid., 36; Aquinas, *Summa Theologica* I-II, q.940 3 ad 3.
36. Ibid., 59, 86–89.
37. Ibid., 101.
38. Ibid., 306.

discounted here, since if having a being-relationship is to be the ground of ethics, that tells us something about ourselves.

As I have already noted, the positivists thought that by paying attention to the use of language they could untangle the problem of ethics. The question what is "good" could be asked by what to we mean by "good." The Oxford philosopher, H. W. B. Joseph, for instance, noted that the "right" is related to a "good."[39] Yet what is the common form of goodness related to all right acts is difficult to see.[40] Joseph concludes that the good is the form of common life.[41]

The problem comes into focus when we link the good to desire.[42] We seem to desire good things, so there relationship between the two. Bond, in *Fact and Value*, provides a useful outline of moral realist position, and is so doing lays bare the problematic relationship between moral objectivity and human desires. He distinguishes a motivating reason (why I desire X) from a grounding reason (which is not internally tied to desires of any kind). He concedes, however, "One is forced to conclude that where value has been discovered a desire exists, but the thing is not good because it is the object of desire—one may desire something when one mistakenly believes it to have value—but because of its actual worth."[43]

As he explains, "rational motivation succeeds, however, in the sense of achieving its end, only when the reason thought to be a reason really is a reason, that is, when the end really is, as it is supposed to be, worth having, getting, and doing."[44] The motivating reason and the grounding reason come together when the object's good cohere with our desires. As he puts it, "Value . . . is not a product of desire, but rather the desire is itself generated by the discovery of value."[45] He said, "Desire satisfaction is neither a necessary or sufficient condition for the recognition of value."[46]

---

39. Joseph, *Some Problems of Ethics*, 37.
40. Ibid., 59.
41. Ibid., 133.
42. Bond, *Reason and Value*, 44.
43. Ibid., 46.
44. Ibid., 56.
45. Ibid., 61, also see 141, 142.
46. Ibid., 146.

A Heideggerian Rebuttal of Ethical Relativism

To avoid problems related to the ontology of values, Bond concedes that values are subject dependent and objective.[47] Goodness, he tells us, belongs to nature as a "felt quality of experience."[48]

Also, once we are no longer convinced of the negative argument, we have a reason to doubt the inductive one in favor of ethical relativism. For Heidegger, we can go much further than remaining sceptical of the ethical relativist conclusion of these arguments. I argued, for him, the actualization of the content of ethical realism inevitable.

Rejecting emotivism requires accepting (1) that values cannot be mind-independent (like pine trees) but (2) somehow attempt to maintain the universality of ethical judgements. Ethical eschatology, in fact, found an expression in Heidegger's tradition, German idealism. Even for Marx, who reacted against German idealism, history comes to an end in the communism republic that gives rise to the ethical state of man. For Heidegger, man comes to himself in a relationship with being.

One reason to be sceptical of ethical relativism, from a Heideggerian point of view, is because it is an expression of scientism that underlies the positivist philosophies. Heidegger, as we have seen, has suggested that ethics will be consequent to having obtained a fundamental relationship to being. I have attempted, in chapters 4–6 and 8, to use, for instance, Maslow and Schweitzer to provide an example of what a fundamental relationship to being could amount to, namely, ethical mysticism.

But we must look to practice to see if any of this so-called mysticism has any connections there. The advice—pay attention to practice—gains currency because of the recent work of a moral philosopher, Williams, who we may wish to recall has provided an important critique of attempts to find the foundations of ethical knowledge.

The following picture emerges. Experience must inform what we think reasonable. We must start with where we find ourselves, with our practices, values, customs, and so on. Also, what counts as reasonable must be open to criticism (in light of intellectual reflection). In order to avoid ethical relativism, criticism must not—as it has, since at least the eighteenth century—supersede our experiences. Further, our experiences arise as cascading dots in the flow to time that does have a terminus, namely according to Heidegger, when we achieve a fundamental relationship with being.

---

47. Ibid., 96.
48. Ibid., 99.

Part III: Contrasts and Reflections

Admittedly, adopting an eschatological ethics, may be a lot to stomach to avoid ethical relativism; my purpose is not so much to convince us to adopt this type of Heideggerian outlook, but to make plain what would be entailed in doing so. In the next chapter, providing a positive argument, I consider to what extent moral realism, to which I have linked Heidegger via an eschatological ethics, is viable.

11

Heidegger and Ethical Naturalism

In the previous chapter, I indicated that we can avoid ethical relativism. In this chapter I will explore, from a neuroscience perspective, how we can embrace moral realism as plausible.

To do so, I turn to recent neurological based insights into the nature of ethics, consider socio-biology, and the *is-ought* split. It may seem odd to bring Heidegger's thought into dialogue with discussions in Anglo-American analytical philosophy, but there already have been wide-ranging attempts to do so within the cognitive sciences.[1]

NEUROETHICS

The first attempts to understand behavior, in the tradition of psychiatry, looked to childhood. Neuroscientists provide a justification for the emphasis on childhood, as a two-year-olds brain contains twice as many synaptic connections as an adult one. At birth we have 100 to 200 billion neurons, and at age two each has 15,000 synapses, more than we will ever have. Synaptic connections are pruned in two ways to make the system more efficient. First, *experience-expectant* pruning occurs during certain development periods when there is an overproduction of synapses, that await stimulation. Areas not stimulated are pruned away. In the first months of life the brain expects visual as well as auditory stimulation, and later language. Second, *experience-dependent* pruning occurs in relation to our individual histories.

1. Winograd and Flores, *Understanding Computers*.

So in a famous study, it was found that London cab drivers have more connections in their hippocampus that plays a key role in special memory. Due to the malleability of the brain, there is the concern that we can to a great extent configure the moral behavior in different ways.

Casebeer, in *Natural Ethical Facts: Evolution, Connectionism, and Moral Cognition*, envisioned a "pragmatic neo-Aristotelian virtue theory, given substantive form by both conceptions of function from evolutionary biology and connectivist conception of thought from cognitive science."[2] He noted that most of the work done in meta-ethics, leaving normative moral theory bereft of content.[3] Citing Flanagan, a well-known philosopher of mind, Casebeer employed the natural method, keeping in mind the pertinent sciences to understand, in this case, ethics, to address the lacuna.[4]

Recall, Moore had claimed that we commit the naturalistic fallacy if we try to define the good. Good cannot be applied to any one object in the world (like sugar), nor our reaction to it. Moore concluded that the good was a non-natural property.[5] We just cannot say what "good" is, rending it a mysterious object of intuition. So the naturalistic fallacy is to attempt to say what goodness is.

Casebeer notes, however, Moore in a new preface for a second edition of *Principia Ethica* understood the mistake, "I [Moore] was, I think, certainly confusing this propositions to the effect that G [Goodness] in not analyzable in one particular way with the proposition that it is not analyzable at all."[6] Citing Boyd, Casebeer suggested goodness is a property cluster (what Boyd calls a homeostatic property cluster) like "healthy."[7]

Casebeer noted that there are a spectrum of views about the relation of science to ethics, two of which concern us, what he calls, the Conservative Unionist (make ethics into science) and Eliminative Unionist (eliminate ethics to science).[8] Suffice it to say, we are at most interested in the more modest aim using science to better understand ethics.

---

2. Casebeer, *Natural Ethical Facts*, 2.
3. Ibid.
4. Ibid., 11.
5. Ibid., 19.
6. Ibid., 21.
7. Ibid., 54.
8. Ibid., 34.

For Plato, noted Casebeer, to know the good is to do it; the motivational force is built in. For Aristotle, pleasure was awareness of an activity; there would be gratification in knowing we are doing the good.[9] The ability to judge is important for learning, and survival, according to Casebeer.[10] The Greeks, however, had a word, *akrasia*, for knowing the good and not doing it.[11] Neurological evidence, further, shows that it is possible to have knowledge of pain, and not wish to avoid it. With lesions to the limbic system we cannot know something is wrong and feel no compulsion to avoid it.[12]

Looking to Narveson's, a Canadian philosopher, suggestion, Casebeer considers the contention that from an evolutionary point of view, once we reproduce, it would not matter what we do, as the main goal is to carry on our genes.[13] Yet we are already, at birth, fitted with the capacity to be imprinted with knowledge, like facial recognition.[14] Casebeer wrote, "To respect morality, then, we must begin by respecting the conditions that enable it to exist."[15] He commented, "Given the normal course of brain ontogeny, moreover, we have good reason to believe that Kant's ideal [to ban emotion from moral judgement] is simply not achievable by any moral cognizer, aside from those with injuries and severe developmental problems."[16]

Casebeer assumes, further, that naturalism entails moral realism.[17] He ends thus: "Living well depends on the reweaving of our ethical theories [and all our beliefs, in fact] into the warp and woof of our scientific heritage, attending to the myriad manifest consequences such a project will have for the way we live our lives and the manner in which we structure our collective moral institutions."[18]

As he went on, "It is—or should be—an effort to come up with a brain-based philosophy of life."[19] Learning about the brain is having dramatic

9. Ibid., 41, 43.
10. Ibid., 92.
11. Ibid., 119.
12. Ibid., 121.
13. Ibid., 65–66.
14. Ibid., 122.
15. Ibid., 132.
16. Ibid., 133.
17. Ibid., 104, 155.
18. Ibid., 161.
19. Gazzaniga, *Ethical Brain*, xv.

resonance with educational theorists, but it can also help us understand philosophical puzzle's about the nature of ethical truths. Emphasizing the social basis of perception and knowledge however carries with it the worry of ethical relativism. Contra Casebeer, naturalism does not by itself dissolve the worry of relativism, but quite the opposite.

When Safile coined "neuroethics" it related to ethical dilemmas that arise in neurology, like brain death. The famous neurologist, Gazzaniga broadens the usage: "As the examination of how we deal with the social issues of disease, normality, morality, lifestyle, and the philosophy of living *informed by our understanding of underlying brain mechanisms.*"[20]

Gazzaniga said that he would like to support the idea that there could be a universal set of biological responses to moral dilemmas, a sort of ethics, built into our brains.[21] The brain uses more neurons to carry out a new task, but once learned, less is needed to process the information, Gazzaniga points out. According to him, the brain whittles down neurons and simplifies the brain response which is automated.[22]

Gazzaniga noted, "It has been found that regions of the brain normally active in emotional processing are activated with one kind of moral judgement but not another."[23] Moral reasoning and brain research deals with three areas: (1) moral emotions (motivating moral behavior), (2) a theory of mind (judging what others think so we can act), and (3), abstract moral reasoning.

There have been attempts to justify a universal ethics, like James Q. Wilson's *The Moral Sense*, however. Gazzaniga noted that for Wilson what is universal is not a law or principle, but the impulse.[24] Gazzaniga wrote, further, "Hauser showed that irrespective of sex, age and culture, most subjects responded in a similar fashion, making similar moral choices."[25]

Hauser argued in *Moral Minds: How Nature Designed our Universal Sense of Right and Wrong* that we evolved a moral instinct. My aim is not to offer a critique of his argument, or any factual errors therein, but only

---

20. Ibid., xv.
21. Ibid., xix.
22. Ibid., 66. As Gazzaniga explained, learning occurs in the synapse, between two neurons. Synapses are made more efficient as the number of neurotransmitters is increased; the synapse surface areas are multiplied; and more synapses are created (75).
23. Ibid., 167.
24. Ibid., 166–67.
25. Ibid., 172.

outline it for our own purposes. He noted that much moral philosophy has stressed judgment, moral principles, and reasoning. Yet he held that much of our reasoning is unconscious. He aimed to explain how our moral intuition works.

There are emotional components to our ethical sensibilities. As Hauser pointed out, we have thought of the distinction, in the Bible, between clean and unclean as moral categories. Even today, we often feel disgust when we hear of moral transgressions. According to him, we make judgements based on considering how our actions affect others, which requires acknowledging they have states of mind and what they are.

As Hauser pointed out, before our first birthday we make inferences based on movement about whether things are living (which are self-moved) or non-living (that must be moved). After fourteen months, he remarked, even eye movement is coordinated where "knowing and feeling" are fused together.[26] According to Hauser we have a "moral acquisition device."[27] He said, "Infants are born with the building blocks for making sense of the causes and consequences of actions, and these early capacities grow and interface with others to generate moral judgements."[28] He contended that what moral system we adopt depends upon our "local culture." We have, he thought, a "universal moral grammar" that is given a variety of different expressions depending upon the social context, though it sets the parameters.[29] He defined, quite generally, the parameters of morality in Rawlsian terms where the idea of fairness figures highly. Hauser endorses a moral pluralism, where no one ethical system reigns supreme, but they are constrained.

It is true that Wilson had already defended the notion of a human nature. Noting that societies are organized around kinship and children, which are not abandoned, he points to the social and pragmatic origin of morality.[30] The neural basis of ethical impulses, must, after all, have served a pragmatic ends if they were to be selected.

Gibbs, in "The EQ Factor," considered emotional intelligence, that is, understanding our feelings, empathy for those of others, and regulating them in a way that enhances living.[31] Primitive emotions, it is reasonable

26. Hauser, *Moral Minds*, 202.
27. Ibid., 303.
28. Ibid.
29. Ibid., 420.
30. Wilson, *Moral Sense*, vii, 15.
31. Gibbs, "EQ Factor," 90.

to think, held the key to survival.³² She tells us that emotional life grows out of the limbic system, specifically the amygdala (also the more connections between the limbic system and neocortex, the greater the amount of emotional responses).³³ Anger causes the release of neurotransmitters called catecholamines. Ninety percent of all emotional communication is nonverbal, and the nervous system is foundational for recognizing and comprehending our environment, especially the social ones.

In a widely cited article, "The Emotional Dog and Its Rational Tail: A Social Intuitionist Approach to Moral Judgement," Haidt argued that reasoning has been overemphasized at the expense of intuition, in the modern history of moral philosophy.³⁴ Moral reasoning, he claimed, is done interpersonally, not privately.³⁵ The fact that psychopaths have moral reasoning, without the accompanying emotions, at least indicates that feelings count.³⁶ All species, he claimed, follow descriptive rules with conspecifics.³⁷ Human infants are unconcerned about fairness till about age four,³⁸ though as young as four a child will talk to a younger sibling of two in a different voice, displaying an empathetic understanding ("I am talking to a baby").

Greene and colleagues, researchers in the Department of Psychology and the Center of the Study of Brain, Mind, and Behavior, at Princeton University, have made some important refinements in the mechanisms that underlie moral behavior and emotions. Their work is remarkable in combining the expertise of neuroscience researchers with the historical perceptiveness of a philosopher.

Greene and associates differentiate a personal moral dilemma from an impersonal one. A personal moral dilemma (1) causes serious bodily harm, (2) befalls a particular person or set thereof, and (3), harm is not deflected from a third party (otherwise it is impersonal).³⁹ They claimed that there is a division in brain functioning dealing with the two types of dilemmas.⁴⁰

---

32. Ibid., 91.
33. Ibid., 91.
34. Haidt, "Emotional Dog," 815.
35. Ibid., 820.
36. Ibid., 824.
37. Ibid., 826.
38. Ibid.
39. Greene et al., "Neural Bases," 2.
40. Ibid., 2.

Cognitive control is often required to override our gut response. Discussing the so-called Stroop task, that is, reading the word "red" written in green ink, they noted takes longer (than if written in red). Our initial response is visual, "green," and we have to override that to read the word as "red." The same interplay occurs between personal and impersonal dilemmas. Greene and associates wrote, "A bilateral increase in amygdale activity for personal, as opposed to impersonal, moral judgements."[41] As they explained, "Difficult personal moral dilemmas, as compared to easy ones, will involve both utilitarian reasoning and (in many cases) the application of cognitive control in favoring utilitarian response over its competitors."[42]

Personal moral judgement involves relatively greater activity in brain areas associated with socio-emotional processing, while impersonal moral judgment involves relatively greater activity in brain areas associated with characteristically "cognitive" processes such as working memory, abstract reasoning, and problem solving.[43]

Greene and associates corroborated (1) the role of emotion and cognition in moral judgement; (2) that "cognitive and emotional processes play crucial and sometimes mutually competitive roles."[44]

As they said, "Utilitarian moral judgement behaviour suggests that cognitive control processes can override these emotional responses, favouring personal moral violations, when the benefits sufficiently out weigh the costs."[45] Yet emotions are never eradicated: "Even a cold, calculated utilitarian must be independently motivated first, to engage in the reasoning that utilitarian judgement requires and, second, to respond in accordance with such judgements: The ACC, a limbic region."[46]

Greene and associates are self-critical, and concede that the emotional (direct motivational force) and cognitive (no direct emotional force) may be a matter of degree.[47] They wrote, "The socio-emotional responses that we've inherited from our primitive ancestors under grid the absolute prohibitions that are central to deontology."[48]

41. Ibid., 5.
42. Ibid., 12.
43. Ibid., 14.
44. Ibid.
45. Ibid., 15.
46. Ibid., 16.
47. Ibid.
48. Ibid.

Should this account prove correct, however, it will have the ironic implication that the Kantian, "rationalist" approach to moral philosophy is, psychologically speaking, grounded not in principles of pure practical reason, but in a set of emotional responses that are subsequently rationalized.[49]

Moll and associates corroborate, in important ways, Greene's and colleagues' research. They wrote, "Recent functional imaging and clinical evidence indicates that a remarkable consistent network of brain regions is involved in moral cognition."[50]

We argue that moral phenomenon emerge from the integration of contextual social knowledge, represented as event knowledge in the prefrontal cortex (PFC); social semantic knowledge, stored in the anterior and posterior cortex; and motivational and basic emotional states, which depend on cortical-limbic circuits.

Moll and associates, interestingly, however, do not presuppose universal moral rules.[51] To kill another person may trigger debate, repulsion, guilt, and so on, but only in certain socio-cultural contexts, where such acts are prohibited. A moral issue, for them, is where we are, or not, in conformity with normative prohibitions. They wrote, "Overall, there is remarkable agreement between functional imagining and clinico-anatomical evidence about brain areas involved in moral cognition."[52] The PFC (prefrontal cortex) has a central role in internalizing moral values and norms from a cultural context.[53] As they explained, "In our view, moral cognitive phenomena emerge from the integration of content—and context dependent representations in cortical-limbic networks."[54]

Berthoz and associates, writing in *NeuroImage*, wrote, "Our working hypothesis is that the amygdala may be crucial for the evaluation of one's social transgression."[55] As they explained, the amygdala, in humans, is involved in the processing and perception of positive or negative stimuli related to preserving well-being. As they noted, "The amygdala could be critically involved in the negative appraisal of a potential threat for the self

---

49. Ibid.
50. Ibid., 1. [Should be Moll?]
51. Moll et al., "Neural Basis," 2.
52. Ibid., 3.
53. Ibid., 8.
54. Ibid., 10.
55. Berthoz et al., "Affective Response," 946.

in the context of one's own wrong doing."⁵⁶ Further, "The amygdala is a crucial part of the neural circuitry by which stimuli trigger emotional responses that reflect the appraisal of value."⁵⁷ The source of the stimuli does not matter; also, the amygdala plays a role in perceiving others emotional states. Intensity of affective response reflects the magnitude of amygdala activity. Berthoz and associates hypothesized that the importance of the amygdala is the punitive relation to reward or punishment, connected to morality.

As they pointed out, the fact that amygdale is activated for personal evaluation corroborates its role in personal welfare.⁵⁸ They wrote, "Guilt is a higher-order, moral emotion considered to arise from one's self's negative evaluation of one's own behaviours or transgressions."⁵⁹ In fact, "Shame also arises from concerns about the effects of one's behaviour on others, and guilt and shame often co-occur."⁶⁰ According to them, guilt relates positively to the development of self at eighteen months and the moral self at fifty-six months.⁶¹

The present finding of its involvement in self-evaluation in relation to social norms suggests the amygdala may also be critical for learning socially appropriate behavior, given that social norms vary across cultures and are learned.⁶²

The Harvard child developmental psychologist, Jerome Kagan created a complex, insightful, and aesthetically brilliant work, *The Nature of the Child*, which, in retrospect, brings into focus neuroethics, and especially the persistent puzzle between moral emotions. He tells us at the second birthday that the child appreciates that her behavior is evaluated by others.⁶³ A motive for task mastery appears.⁶⁴

56. Ibid.
57. Ibid., 948.
58. Ibid., 949.
59. Ibid.
60. Ibid.
61. Ibid.
62. Ibid.
63. Kagan, *Nature of the Child*, 6.
64. As Kagan noted, the fact a child gets bored of a pleasurable acts, popping balloons, indicates we know something about it. A child, further, tries to maintain consistency in belief and action.

Part III: Contrasts and Reflections

According to Kagan, our beliefs change, but those that are resistant to doing so are called a "frame."[65] He wrote, "The central element in Piaget's theory of the infant is the sensory-motor schema. It is a representation of the class of motor actions necessary to obtain a goal, and it is acquired through active manipulation of objects."[66]

Yet there are also innate dispositions rooted in the maturation of the nervous system, according to Kagan: absence of a caregiver (at a given age); fear of novel events.[67] Corroborating the earlier work of Harlow, he notes that squirrel monkeys show higher levels of cortisol in the absence of mothers, even when they behave normally.[68]

Yet Kagan noted that a secure attachment, at one year, will not be beneficial indefinitely.[69] As Kagan explained, "Each child's temperament leads him or her to impose a special frame on experience, thus making it difficult to predict the consequences of a particular home environment."[70]

Kagan noted that a four-year-old child will morally evaluate their dreams, feeling perhaps guilty of thinking something bad.[71] According to Kagan, after the fourth birthday the child believes they have a choice, giving rise to the consistency in beliefs.[72] The first phase in establishing a self, in fact, Kagan noted, is awareness of goals, standards, and intentions, as well as the ability to obtain them.[73] By three, a child can appreciate different age roles.[74]

Kagan wrote, "One four-year-old asked his mother if a person who dies can get another person's bones and become alive again. Piaget

---

65. Ibid., 8.
66. Ibid., 48.
67. Ibid., 45, 47.
68. Ibid., 61.
69. Ibid., 63.

70. Ibid., 70. Drawing on an unpublished PhD dissertation of Vidal (1981), submitted at Harvard, Kagan wrote that it was Piaget's study of snails, where he argued that morphological changes occur over time, in commerce with the environment, then encoded, that would shape his entire work.

71. Ibid., 129.
72. Ibid., 135.
73. Ibid., 138.

74. Sparrows singing and rats rubbing their whiskers are behaviors, said Kagan, rooted in their central nervous system, requiring no experience. The maturation of the brain is linked to changing mental functions, which in turn allow shaping of the neural system.

nominated this competence as the most essential in his theory of cognitive development."[75] Commenting, Kagan noted, Piaget was a pragmatist; knowledge has a purpose.[76] A feature of a category that is shared most will become salient. As Kagan explained in the category *animal* the notion of *domestic animal* is important for rural children, but not so for urban ones.[77]

Yet the distinction between the context in which competencies are activated, Kagan remarked, hides a distinction between (1) cognitive competence and (2), public performance.[78] The social context of learning is omnipresent. In fact, creative children, Kagan said, search for the unusual; delight in novel ideas; and are not apprehensive about making mistakes.[79] In a comparison between creative architects from ones that are only successful we find: a premium on originality; solitary work; and less thought about others.[80]

The central moral of Kagan's work is that it is not what happens to us that count, but how we interpret it.[81] Even the assumed givens—we need a stable child-mother relationship—are not so, Kagan remarked. Mayan men, who have stable relations in childhood, are suspicious and aggressive towards their wives. Without stable relations, we may have successful relations. The malleability, and adaptability of the brain, in relation to a cultural context, complicates locating the genesis of the moral instinct. Still, we may hold out hope that there are some limits to human behavior that would fall within the purview of an ethics.

Contending that temperament is shaped in early childhood, Wright, in "Brains, Bonds, and Babies," wrote, "A child's brain remains surprisingly malleable months and even years after birth."[82] Children, she noted, are sensitive to cues from parents, especially indifference.[83] She wrote, "Developmental psychologists now believe that bonding with a parent or other

75. Ibid., 189.
76. Ibid., 190.
77. Ibid., 217.
78. Ibid., 198.
79. Ibid., 222.
80. Ibid.
81. Ibid., 240–41. Our society is distinct Kagan noted with the emphasis upon independence; the value attributed to romantic love; and the celebration of freedom (244–45, 272).
82. Wright, "Babies, Bonds, and Brains," 84.
83. Ibid., 85.

Part III: Contrasts and Reflections

caregiver is essential to normal childhood as learning to walk and talk."[84] Driving, making music, reading, and so on, all shape the brain in a unique way, as does our emotional experiences.

Harlow' experiments with rhesus monkeys, in the late fifties (though disturbing) showed that the infants raised with a wire mesh prosthetic mother were more disturbed than those with a cloth one. Those whose early bonding requirements are not met are: (i) fearful to explore new objects; (ii) aggressive, maladjusted to social setting; (iii) hyper-oral (thumb-sucking); (iv) the lower levels of serotonin (a biochemical mood-regulator linked to aggression, antisocial behavior, and depression in humans); (v) suppressed immune system; (vi) level of stress hormones are higher (cortisol) in tense situations; (vii) learning difficulties: lowered attention span, learning, and memory.[85] Wright comments that even those with inborn tendencies can avoid anxiety, if raised by ultra-caring mothers.

The neural rationale is that the primitive areas of the brain, like the limbic system, mature first (where emotional information is processed). The frontal cortex, which governs planning and decision making, and cerebellum, a center for motor skills, and is involved in emotional development, at age five to seven. Major restructuring of the brain occurs again between the ages of nine to eleven, and some reorganization occurs every two years.[86] Wright said, "Long-term studies are just now beginning to demonstrate that experiences later in life can redirect behavioural and emotional development, even in adulthood."[87]

An important conference was held at Washington State University in St. Louis and the articles have been subsequently published, *Mind and Morals*. Writing for the conference, David and A. J. Premack, considered the development of morality in children, assume that it is concerned with social behavior. The social assumption is useful insofar as leads them to look at the social context in which morality develops. According to them, infants distinguish between something moving another thing, and when it is self-propelled.[88] To move something else is to have power over it (to possess it).[89] As Paul Churchland, the philosopher of mind, noted, "What

84. Ibid.
85. Ibid.
86. Ibid., 87.
87. Ibid.
88. Premack and Premack, "Moral Belief," 149–50.
89. Ibid., 155.

I do wish to assert is that in learning to represent the world, the brain of infant social creatures focus naturally and relentlessly on the social features of their local environment."[90]

Most of our neural processing, on a daily basis, is about judging our relations to other people—these are often power issues. Relating to basic needs, like safety, it would be important to judge our situation in a social context.

As we have made a few remarks about infants, let us turn our attention to the opposite end of the spectrum, the adult psychopath. Deigh, in "Empathy and Universalizability" conducts an interesting reflection on those adults that lack the moral sense. Though psychopathy is often defined as the lack of conscience or accompanying moral feeling, there is sometimes a display of selective empathy for family or friends. Nevertheless, according to Deigh, the psychopath can be characterized by (i) inability to enter into relationships, (ii) lack of empathy, (iii) low self-esteem often expressed as self-aggrandizement, (iv) a confusion of the sexual instinct with power to an extreme degree, (v) an attempt to compensate for low self-esteem by attention seeking.[91]

Scheman has considered moral feelings in relation to objectivity, and wrote, emotions "identity as complex entities is relative to explanatory schemes that rely on social meaning and interpretation."[92] She emphasized that emotions are social and inform moral judgements.[93]

At a crude level, pain is not social. Yet emotions, more generally, do relate to an entire socio-cultural world, of hopes, wants, expectations, which in turn, are rooted in our sense of well-being. Writing for the same conference, Bratman explained, "Much of our behaviour is organized. It is organized over time within the life of the agent, and it is organized interpersonally."[94]

We have connections to Heidegger. Emphasizing upon the role of emotions in moral behavior, in any case, neuro-ethicists give credence to Heidegger's strategy, as I have outlined it. Though moral reasoning is indispensable, it rests upon more primitive sets of emotions, which are the result of some five millions years of hominid evolution. The perennial criticism of

---

90. Churchland, "Neural Representation," 99.
91. Deigh, "Empathy and Universalizability," 200.
92. Scheman, "Feeling Our Way," 222.
93. Ibid., 230.
94. Bratman, "Planning and Temptation," 293.

Part III: Contrasts and Reflections

Kant's formalism, from all corners, gains weight. The contention that we do not decide ethical matters the way Kant outlined, led some to claim he offered a rational reconstruction of ethics, not a justification but description of what we do. For a naturalist however what we do must cohere with how we justify knowledge, in principle.

Heidegger is often taken to emphasize that we occupy different worlds. With the rise of anthropology, ethical relativism looms large. All perception is shaped by social factors to some degree. Words do not just denote, but connote. Considering something *clean* or *unclean*, the language of the old religions, had moral connotations. Speaking of a different "universe," as Casebeer did is, however, to exaggerate the problem of ethical relativism, which is one of various social constructions. Once again, the moral is the same: ethics is something normative in the social sense, but also psychologically. Those that do not follow ethical norms are somehow missing something, which I suggest, in part, are ethical feelings. In this book, I have contended that there are perhaps some certain moral fundamentals, like fairness, that are universal. The social context gives life to moral sentiments in relation to diverse environmental and social conditions.

Hauser's picture is consistent with the Heideggerian picture I have attempted to develop. There are certain innate dispositions providing for empathy and a sense of fairness that provide the basis for any morality whatsoever. Morality grows out of development; it requires both sentiments and reasoning, leading to judgement. We develop to survive in a social context that itself must negotiate with realities of the past, present, and future.

Unlike the Heideggerian picture I advocate, however, Hauser's endorsement of pluralism pays homage to the diversity of ethical systems. I have suggested, pace Heidegger, we must consider moral development as running on a parallel track with the unfolding of the history of being. The problem has been that we have sit, according to Heidegger, at an orthogonal juncture as we stray from our ideal nature. Various moral systems, if inscribed, are records of the consequences of our negotiations with fellows, including our cumulative tradition, environment, and inherited dispositions. Under appropriate conditions, to which we find ourselves on the way, we may have a fuller realization of our ethical destiny.

A naturalist account of brain evolution supports the notion that there are better or worse moral systems in which we may be inculcated. It should be no surprise if the brain developed first to process our relationship to a social environment, which included affective response and that emotions play a role in moral reasoning. Yet it is emotions that have been spurned by moral philosophers.

Plato was almost right in *The Republic*. The notional state is the brain writ large. Like a house, we have the foundational sentiments that are regulated by the upper floors, the prefrontal cortex (PFC). The entire debate between the heart and mind, as well as various philosophical movements, like romanticism and rationalism, find a neural basis and bias.

With Haidt's article a debate began in the neuroscience literature that brought us back to Hume, with a twist. Rational (ethical) acts must rest on the passions. Yet it is not obvious that the passions are themselves irrational. The passions may also have a justification within the context of a natural scientific account of human moral behavior.

I have contended that for Heidegger, the being-experience may be part of a rational reconstruction of ethical knowledge, in the introduction. Insofar, however, that the being-experience helps us understand the moral emotions and behaviors we already engage in, it provides a rationale and reinforcement for them. Humans need to understand why we do what we do. Habit, disposition rooted in our evolutionary heritage, is not enough. My conjecture is that the being-experience is a sophisticated one—rendering intelligible our emotions and behaviors in relation to our culture, mediated by historical reflection—which probably requires the PFC, and has emotional resonance in the amygdala.

Greene and associates recognized that there was an ambiguity between what counts as an emotion and reason. The ambiguity between emotion and reason is reflected in the history of moral philosophy in trying to distinguish Kantian deontology from rule utilitarianism, both of which require taking the perspective of the abstract agent delegating universal moral rules. Though the neural research, of itself, does not determine the realist debate, evidenced by the fact that various neuroethicists like Gazzanaga, on the one hand, and Moll and associates on the other, demonstrate.

The following picture is at least plausible: ethical reasoning is based upon values rooted in primitive emotions. Yet underneath those emotions are the global reasons—that is, we organize to survive in an environment, which has left its marks on the evolution of the brain.

Part III: Contrasts and Reflections

Table 3
"The Relationship between Individual Ethical Acts and the Social Context"

Individual rationale ↓	Individual action ←
Emotions ↓	↑ Brain ontogeny
Global rationale →	↑ Organizational behavior

The upshot is that emotions are not banned, as traditional readings of Kant had required. Rather, Heidegger's rereading of Kant gains neurological support. At the basis of the Kantian moral system is respect. We need both reasoning and emotions (which motivate moral behavior) and they are linked, in broad outline, between the PFC and amygdala. The importance of the amygdala, I emphasize, is that it is linked to social relations and our welfare.

The following picture of the neurological basis of ethics is at least plausible. The prefrontal cortex is important for planning and reasoning necessary for regulating impulses and emotions. It takes till the teenage years till the prefrontal cortex is fully functional. We need to have empathetic sentiments that are processed in the amygdala. We also need to be able to negotiate our own self interested needs within a plan that takes into account the consequences. What is considered an ethical consequence worthy of empathy is partly socially determined but often based in primitive ethical sentiments. There must be a communication, as it were, between the emotional and rational processing modules of the brain to yield a conscience. What Heidegger offers, prospectively, is a reconstruction of the disparate ways we have constructed ourselves, as well as an account that suggests that some ways are better than others. The being-relationship is meta-cognitive experience that offers insight into our relationship with the world in terms of a moral vision of kinship and interdependence.

Philosophers, in probing the foundation of ethics, have often focused on the agent or objects, which conceals the social context in the formation of the self. Heidegger's analytic of Dasein forces us to locate ourselves in-a-world.

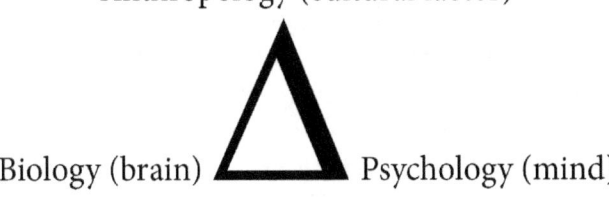

Figure 1

THE SOCIO-CULTURAL ASPECT OF DASEIN

Extending Dewey's pragmatism, we engage in inquiry is to solve problems, or because the tradition in which we participate aims to do so. The social context (often missing in the above picture) drives research as well as ethics.

Kagan, as well as other child and social psychologists, emphasizing the connection between context, history, and evolution in relation to the nervous system, do not keep us far from the philosophical puzzle of ethical relativism. In postmodern Heideggerian jargon, we never escape the world we are in. We need a reply to the moral relativist. I now turn to consider the greatest attempt in the twentieth century to found a science of ethics, sociobiology, which had fallen into disrepute because of the threat of ethical relativism. I shall seek to defend sociobiology, as its fate, in a peculiar way, is caught up with Heidegger's style of moral realism.

The classic example of using science to justify ethics is ecological behaviorism (previously called sociobiology). E. O. Wilson wrote, "Sociobiology is the systematic study of the biological basis of all social behaviour."[95] Sociobiology has been thought philosophically untenable because of the *is-ought* problem, which was identified by David Hume. Wilson, furthermore, deems it the most important philosophical problem for sociobiology.[96]

Since the sociobiologist only describes what *is* the case, so the charge goes, she cannot, in principle, justify what *ought* to be the case.[97] For in-

---

95. MacArthur and Wilson, *Theory of Island Biogeography*, 4; Kitcher, *Vaulting Ambition*, 394.

96. Hume, *Treatise on Human Nature* 3.1.1.27 (his work was originally published in 1739); Kitcher, "Psychological Altruism," 309–10. Wilson said, "The challenge to science and philosophy to solve this dilemma of *is-ought* is very great—in our opinion, there is none greater" (Lumsden and Wilson, *Promethean Fire*, 183).

97. Lumsden and Wilson, *Promethean Fire*, 183; Kitcher, *Vaulting Ambition*, 430.

Part III: Contrasts and Reflections

stance, if we were living during the time of slavery in the United States, sociobiologists would seem to have explain such oppressive behavior in evolutionary terms as shaping both groups (the slaves and the owners). The sociobiologist, so the charge goes, lacks any point from which to criticize any one specific ethical system (say one that includes the practice of slavery) precisely because we are deriving what ought to be the case from what is so. Furthermore, if the *is* and *ought* are co-extensive, and the *is* changes, ethical relativism seems confirmed by anthropological evidence.

Recall, ethical relativism is the idea that ethical statements' truth and falsity are indexed to changing standards (or points of view). Conversely, moral realism is the idea that ethical statements are determinately true or false. For the moral realist, we can be wrong about what we think constitutes correct behavior.

W. V. O. Quine, towards the end of his famous paper "Naturalized Epistemology" conjectures that evolution may help clarify induction, now that we are allowing epistemology the resources of natural science.[98] Naturalized epistemology is the notion that we can use science to help justify its methodologies. Science is incredibly successful when applied to the world. In the short term, at least, it has helped the human specie survive.[99] Kitcher has suggested that naturalized epistemology, like that envisioned by Quine, can aid the sociobiologist.[100] In what follows, I attempt to demonstrate how a naturalized epistemological can solve the *is-ought* problem; that is, how we can be a naturalists and realists about ethics.

According to Wilson, there are similarities between insect and vertebrate societies (his early and later work, respectively). Mathematical models of the relationship between the environment, social behavior, and genes, in insects, are to be extended to vertebrates.[101] That is, the models used to explain the genetic basis of the behavior of relatively simple organisms is to be extended to more complex ones.

The story goes like this: Genes delimit abilities, which, in turn, circumscribe cultural possibilities and behavior. Wilson envisions that the genetic mechanisms that influence, for instance, human behavior, are, in

---

98. Quine, *Ontological Relativity*, 90.

99. Wilson wrote, "Evolution can be broadly defined as any change in the genetic constitution of a population. Population genetics has allowed a more precise definition: Any change in gene frequency (Wilson and Bossert, *Primer of Population Biology*, 20).

100. Quine, *Ontological Relativity*; Kitcher, "Psychological Altruism," 306.

101. Wilson, *Insect Societies*, 485.

turn, also affected by what we do. Wilson claims that preferred behaviors can leave their genetic imprint.

Thus, according to Wilson, Lamarck's idea that behavior can effect one's genetic constitution was incorrect in the life of the individual, but not in the case of the group over generations.[102] We can put aside the case of epigenetic effects, whereby what an organism does during its lifespan can have genetic consequences for its progeny. Most efforts we make during our life, for example, lifting weights or practicing mathematics, will have no biological consequences (in the sense under consideration) for our offspring. Our offspring will not be stronger or better at doing mathematics. Yet what the group does, in terms of behavior, matters biologically. If being good at mathematics increases our chance of surviving, the genes that increase that ability may be selected.

Consider an example from the non-human animal kingdom. Starlings fly close together when there is a hawk above but not below. The starlings' movements could remain unchanged, fly haphazardly apart, and so on. Yet flying close together make it harder for a hawk to prey upon one of the starlings without injuring itself.[103] On a sociobiological account the genetic trait that disposes starlings to fly close together when faced with a hawk above has been genetically selected. The following picture emerges:

Table 4
"From Genes to Behavior"

Genes	Ability	Culture	Behavior
A	B	C	D

In a nutshell, A, genes support and enhance the winning strategy shall be reproduced if an only if, D, a group adopts a pattern of behavior that aids in its survival. The relationship between biology and behavior is an evolutionary two-way street.[104] Biology determines what behaviors are possible and disposes organisms to some of them. Behavior, in turn, can shape, over

---

102. Incidentally, Darwin did not have a concept for the unit, the gene that explains the mechanism of natural selection.

103. MacArthur and Wilson, *Theory of Island Biogeography*, 39, 476.

104. Lumsden and Wilson, *Genes, Minds, and Culture*, 250.

generations, the biological profile of organisms. Epigenetics may only further reinforce ethical or non-ethical dispositions.

Applying the general two-way street picture to human beings is difficult. Humans' evolutionary advantage is flexibility (we can learn different types of behavior depending on prevailing environmental conditions). Yet if we are ethical realists, there are things (some ethical fundamentals) that shall be invariable, at least as values present in all cultures. On a sociobiological account, ethics must in part be accounted for biologically, say, as some set of dispositions.[105] Furthermore, Wilson did contend that sociobiology can account for ethics. Yet Wilson is not sure if sociobiology leads to relativism.[106]

So far, I have dwelt on outlining how the *is-ought* problem arises and what the sociobiological program is about. We also need to understand a bit of the background of the naturalist program, however, to see if we can find a solution to the *is-ought* problem. I turn to naturalism.

The naturalist program, as conceived by Quine, depends on two arguments, one negative and one positive.[107] The negative argument is against first philosophy. The positive argument is a scientific account of the acquisition of basic concepts. Traditional, foundational epistemology (first philosophy) is the idea that knowledge can be justified on a model akin to an axiomatic system like that of Euclid. On the foundational model, upon a finite number of first principles (the conceptual) rests knowledge (the doctrinal).

Also, since at least Frege, who has been influential in shaping how we have thought about traditional epistemology, there is a difference of the context of discovery from that of justification. How we acquire the values, practices, and knowledge (the doctrinal) said nothing about their epistemic justification.[108]

First, however, for a naturalized epistemologist, the distinction between the context of discovery from justification is rejected. Frege's assumption is thrown out. The context of discovery can speak to the issue of justification, provided we pay attention to the case in question. In some cases justification is divorced from discovery. For example, the mathematization of electro-magnetic theory by Maxwell served as a corroboration

---

105. Ibid., 549.
106. Ibid., 129.
107. Gibson, "Quine on Naturalizing Epistemology," 89.
108. Frege, *Foundations of Arithmetic*, § 3.

(of electro-magnetic theory). Yet Maxwell's mathematization played no role in the discovery of electro-magnetic theory. Justification, regarding the mathematization of the theory, is divorced from the discovery of electro-magnetic theory. We can identify features of discovery play no role in justification. For example, and more generally, hitting our head on the bathtub may be the way we discovered X, but that would not count as the justification for X.

Yet, there are the cases of interest to the naturalist, where certain features of discovery play a role in justification. For example, in the case of basic arithmetic, the logic of discovery (e.g., as explained by Kitcher in *The Nature of Mathematical Knowledge*) is supposed to be, more or less, isomorphic with justification. That is, Kitcher's account of how basic arithmetic is acquired is also to speak to its justification. Kitcher can explain why we all have the same arithmetic: We all interact with the world with the same anatomical apparatus.

Second, according to a naturalized epistemologist, we begin with epistemic content, e.g., science. Empirical psychology is to explain how we acquire basic concepts, which serve as the foundation of knowledge. There is still what is foundational (i.e., acquired, basic concepts) and what rests upon that (the doctrinal).[109]

For a naturalized epistemologist, it is a truism that we are justifying the epistemic content of the day. On a pragmatist account like that of one of the founders of the view, Peirce, however, since science is an ongoing, self-correcting enterprise, epistemic relativism is avoided.[110] Truth is what would not be overturned at the ideal end of inquiry.[111]

As I have hinted, Quine's naturalism not only prompts one to re-look at sociobiology but also contains the prima materia from which to respond to its greatest threat: The *is-ought* problem. It is worth keeping in mind that it has not been my purpose, however, to offer any substantive defence for the naturalist rejection of foundationalism or the idea of an ideal end of inquiry.

Rather, I wish to expose a strategy. Namely, by accepting the pragmatist's tack, a naturalist can solve the *is-ought* problem. Sociobiology is consistent with ethical realism. We may remain optimistic that ethics is not completely beyond scientific investigation. I have suggested we have a right

---

109. Frassen, "Against Naturalized Epistemology," 81.
110. Sellars, *Empiricism*, 79.
111. Misak, *Truth and the End of Inquiry*, 124.

to be optimistic because, all other options considers, science is the strong card. As Putnam, another pragmatist, said more generally, "Science at best is a way of coming to know, and hopefully a way of acquiring some reverence for, the wonders of nature."[112] If ethics is one of the wonders of nature, then science should have something to say about it.

Kitcher, a defender of naturalism in mathematics, once held that biological genealogy does not affect philosophical debates in meta-ethics or substantiative normative debates. He criticized sociobiology in *Vaulting Ambition: Sociobiology and the Quest for Human Nature*.[113] His criticisms have helped refine sociobiology and render it more plausible.

Kitcher claims, for instance, that by clarifying the methodological standards that the discipline ought to meet "may even help us to envisage the *future* development of an approach to human behaviour that makes genuine use of biological insights."[114] It is worth getting a picture of what revised sociobiology will look like.

Kitcher remarked on several problems:

1. Evolution may justify a might is right ethics, which leads to eugenics.[115]

2. There is no evidence for the idea that there is a genetic basis for specific social, human customs.[116]

3. The biological evidence there is for a custom, does not support only the sociobiological hypothesis (e.g., just because we are genetically disposed to be social, we can also work together to plunder and pillage).[117]

4. Sociobiology conflicts with what agents purport to be doing, i.e., acting freely.[118]

5. The sociobiological hypothesis is not falsifiable.[119]

---

112. Putnam, *Mathematics, Matter, Method*, 1:xiv.

113. Kitcher, *Vaulting Ambition*, ix, 54.

114. Ibid., ix.

115. The fundamental theorem of natural selection: "The rate of evolution is proportional to the genetic variance of the population" (Wilson and Bossert, *Primer of Population Biology*, 79).

116. Wilson, *Insect Societies*, 485.

117. MacArthur and Wilson, *Theory of Island Biogeography*, 24, 28.

118. Kitcher, "Evolution of Human Altruism," 507.

119. Wilson, *Sociobiology*, 22.

6. Sociobiology may not be able to account for altruism.[120]

7. We cannot derive the *ought* from the *is*.

Suffice it to say that many problems can, in principle, be responded to, with emendations, that give rise to a revised sociobiology; in a nutshell, a revised sociobiology is to contribute to uncovering the dispositions that underlie ethics, but rids itself of the burden of uncovering the genetic mechanisms that are exclusively responsible for ethical behavior. It is at least plausible to think that a revised sociobiology could address many of the concerns that Kitcher raises.

Kitcher, more recently, said that biological genealogy does have meta-ethical implications.[121] He wrote: "More promising than traditional sociobiology is the thought that we can learn important things about the nature of morality by conceiving of ourselves as part of the natural order, that part of meta-ethics—particularly moral metaphysics and moral epistemology—should be re-configured through explicit recognition of the fact that our practices and precepts have long histories and that those histories eventually terminate on the savannah in the psychological dispositions of our remote ancestors and in the kinds of social arrangements that fashioned them."[122] Even once we delimit the scope of sociobiology, seeking out dispositions for ethical behavior, the *is-ought* problem remains. That is, a revised sociobiology still requires tackling the *is-ought* problem.

Yet once we adopt a naturalized outlook, sociobiology can aid in describing the process by which we have arrived at the ethics we have (where we assume we have the correct ethics, or something pretty close). Furthermore, some of the reasons to adopt naturalized epistemology in the first place (e.g., an exasperation with foundational epistemology) is likely to resonate with the sociobiologist. As Dennett put it, "If 'ought' cannot be

---

120. Kitcher, *Vaulting Ambition*, 399. Extreme altruism is "self-destructive behavior performed for the benefit of others" (Wilson, *Insect Societies*, 321)—can be accounted for in social insects by sociobiologists. Hamilton working from traditional axioms of population genetics deduced the following principle that applies to any genotype: "In order for an altruistic behaviour to evolve, the sacrifice of fitness by an individual must be compensated for by an increase in some group of relatives by a factor greater than the reciprocal of the coefficient of the relationship to the group. The coefficient of relationship is the equivalent of the average fraction of genes shared by common descent; thus in sisters it is one-half; in half-sisters one-fourth; in first cousins, one-eighth, and so on" (ibid., 320).

121. Kitcher, "Psychological Altruism," 306.

122. Ibid., 283.

derived from 'is' just what can 'ought' be derived from? Is ethics an *entirely* 'autonomous' field of inquiry? Does it float untethered to facts from any other discipline or tradition?... The most compelling answer is this: ethics must be *somehow* based on an appreciation of human nature—on a sense of what a human being is or might be, and on what a human being might want to have or want to be. If *that* is naturalism, then naturalism is no fallacy.[123]

Dennett is on to something. Describing what *is* the case only entails relativism if we assume that it is in conflict with a universalist ethic. Yet there are three ways the relationship between the *is* and *ought* can be configured (which, respectively, result in three distinctive consequences for ethics). Each must be considered. First, is the pessimistic case: *is-ought* conflict. If a sociobiological account can only tell us what *is* the case (and not how *ought* to be the case) it can merely describe different regimes of ethical governance, each perhaps best suited to the environment in which they arose. Sociobiology entails ethical relativism. We cannot derive *ought* from *is*.

The second position is agnosticism: scepticism about the conflict between the *is-ought*. Agnosticism is the idea that we remain sceptical about the conflict and uses naturalism to describe, but not justify, our ethics at the time. Sociobiology has no consequences for resolving philosophical debates about moral realism. Sociobiology merely helps explain different regimes of ethical governance.

Finally, we may be optimistic: The *is* and *ought* are co-extensive. Optimism idea that by describing how we acquired an ethics, aids in its justification; there is no conflict between sociobiology and ethics. Optimism perhaps requires a metaphysical commitment, e.g., a belief that it is the best of all possible worlds, since we have to assume the emergence of an environment that will promote genetic dispositions consistent with ethical behavior.[124] That is, we are forced to be optimistic about our ethical eschatology. For example, being a realist about a specific set of ethical fundamentals (say, the United Nations *Declaration of Human Rights*), requires assuming that the eschatology of moral inquiry has, to some extent, come to an end, or at the very least is moving in the right direction. The naturalist committed to ethical realism must believe that the universe will give rise to an environment that will lead to the selection of behaviors imprinted as biological traits that support ethics.

123. Dennett, *Darwin's Dangerous Idea*, 467–68.
124. Lumsden and Wilson, *Promethean Fire*, vi.

Naturalized epistemology offers two ways to render the threat from the *is-ought* distinction innocuous, both of which require optimism. First, Quine's naturalism offers a precedent (from the domain of science) of ruling out the need to provide a knock-down argument against the ethical relativist (since that is impossible). To adopt Quine's phraseology, once we have stopped dreaming of justifying moral imperatives in our head alone, evolutionary theory may make a useful contribution, provided we begin with some ethical content.

A naturalist can be sceptical of this or that bit of science but not the entire enterprise all at once. Global scepticism is ruled out. Similarly, to follow the analogy, we can be sceptical about this or that bit of ethical knowledge, but not reject the entire enterprise per se (as the relativist seems to do). In a nutshell, we avoid ethical relativism by beginning with some moral content and work backwards to justify it. The justification for beginning with some moral content is largely negative: foundational ethics leads to a quagmire of scepticism in the same way that its epistemic brethren do for scientific knowledge, and that, for a pragmatist, is untenable. According to the naturalist, we are advised to begin with some epistemic content and explain how it is constructed.

Second, another tactic, for the naturalist, is to claim that the *ought* is manifest at the end of moral inquiry. According to a naturalized epistemologist there is nothing deeper than the story of how we attained the practices-cum-knowledge we have. If the analogy from science is to be followed (where knowledge seems to be improving) we are led to conclude that we are participating in ethical evolution. That is, the changing faces of *is* are all closer approximations of the *ought*. Arguing about one *ought* to do, social progress, or dialogue in general, is not precluded. Rather, a description of the process by which one acquires ethics, which may require debate and disagreement, is included in its justification.

The slogan: *is* includes *ought*. That is, evolutionary theory can justify the process by which we reject some behavior and institute others. Collectively, the naturalist may contend that human societies have a moral trajectory upon which they shall converge. Also, it is not clear why Moore's thought was to discourage the scientific investigation of the good; we could consider intuition from a cognitive science point of view. Objects need not exist in physical time and space (like numbers) to be worthy of the realists attention. Naturalism in ethics is no fallacy, suffice it to say.

Part III: Contrasts and Reflections

Two paths have been outlined by which to disarm the *is-ought* problem: (1) start with some ethical content, or (2) assume that the changes in the moral life of society are heading towards a final destination. The two paths are not mutually exclusive. As is the case with naturalists' orientation towards science, we may want to maintain the necessity of certain facts while allowing that new ones may be added or some old ones refined (or refuted). The same may be true for the ethical naturalist who wishes to be a moral realist. Some moral facts held today are resistant to change and others are evolving.

The challenge of ethical relativism is crystallized, in the philosophical tradition, in the is-ought distinction, which I have argued, Heidegger via pragmatists can address. As with emotions, the spade has to turn somewhere. Providing a picture, pragmatists provide an avenue for the Heideggerian to achieve moral realism. Heidegger, in fact, embraces change, and assumes it has a trajectory, the ethical realization of Dasein. In the next chapter I present my conclusions.

12

Prospects for Moral Realism

In this chapter, I aim to consolidate our understanding of the content, shape, and plausibility of a Heideggerian ethics. I shall summarize my findings and reflect upon their implications.

I applied Heidegger's critique of the history of Western philosophy to ethics. I showed that is possible, and plausible, to read Heidegger as a metaphysician. As students of ethics, it was suggested how Heidegger's concentration on the being-relationship (*Bezug zum Seyn*) could provide the ground of an environmentally friendly ethics, also. The being-relationship, as he suggests, can be the basis of an ethics. Here is how I developed this idea.

In part I, I considered Heidegger's overall view in more detail. In chapter 1, I argued that there are positive links to metaphysics in Heidegger's thought. Heidegger's latter writings point us to a retrieval of a more original metaphysics, for which he turns our attention towards the pre-Socratics.

In chapter 2, I attempted to explain what Heidegger had indicated in his early work; our ethic will be determined by our relationship to being. What justifies ethics for Heidegger is metaphysics.

In chapter 3, I considered Heidegger's reading of Kant. From Heidegger's reading of Kant, in order to develop the notion that a Heideggerian ethic is aimed at accounting for the motivation of ethics. Heidegger's reading of Kant, for instance, beckons us to begin with the practice of ethics. Kant, however, draws a wall between what justifies ethics and what motivates it. The cornerstone of a Heideggerian ethic is the rejection of Kant's assumption. What justifies ethics, must also motivate it.

In chapter 4, I considered the romantic motivations behind Heidegger's program, and how this led him into two distinct types of problems. He viewed National Socialism as the solution to the problems of the modern world. Heidegger's politics, I suggested, however, led himself to contradiction on several points—for example, his duplicitous views about German science and technology. Philosophically, the question of being, as he understood it, seems to be vacuous, too. I argued that we can defend Heidegger from by separating his philosophy from his politics and reading him as a mystic.

Also, by way of drawing parallels to Spengler, I locate Heidegger in the Romantic Movement. I explain, from a Heideggerian perspective, how ethical subjectivism came to flourish with the loss of a fundamental relationship to being in modernity. I exposed, more importantly for my investigation, what morally realist consequences may be entailed in a recovery of a fundamental relationship to being. To provide detail to the nature of the experience of being, I turned to Maslow's idea of peak experiences, what he calls Being-cognition. Through Being-cognition we likely achieve self-actualization, higher up on Maslow's hierarchy of needs, dealing with safety, security, and belonging.

In part II, I delved further into what the question of being could mean, since it is upon that which ethics is supposed to find its footing, for Heidegger. In chapter 5, I showed that it remains unclear what the question of being could mean even once we convert that into a question about primordial time. In fact, we are tempted to ask if the *everyday* is not as much a chimera as the sense data of the British empiricists. Or at least, where does returning to everyday practices get us philosophically? For Heidegger, I argue, the story goes like this.

In chapter 6, I consider, and argue that Heidegger favors what I dubbed ontological similarity. I attempted to show, in a nutshell, that it is plausible to understand the question of being, and more generally to read Heidegger, in mystical terms, whereby beings and being are held together in some sort of unison.

In part III, in order to make a Heideggerian ethic a convincing option, I considered various points of contrast and comparison to Heidegger. For example, in chapter 7, I considered Kant's ethical program; I explain how Heidegger can remedy some standard complains with Kant's ethics.

Prospects for Moral Realism

In chapter 8, I turned our attention to Hegel's aesthetics, whereby art provides an experience that allows us to access truth; in short, our experience of such a cultural artifact provides a window into the unfolding of the absolute idea in history. Hegel, in his own way, was able to resolve the chasm between particulars and universals, thus solving the problem of ontological difference. The parallel to Heidegger are telling, where he seeks some kind of experience of being (like an experience of art) to underpin his ethics. Also, I have sought to explain how he can account for how we can have various epochs with different ethics and still be a moral realist. Hegel provides the clue: the end of history (a point taken up in chapters 10–11).

In chapter 9, I considered Schweitzer's metaphysical ethics, which I argue, could be illustrative of a Heideggerian ethic. I have attempted to explain how a fundamental relationship to being, for example, could be the foundation of ethics, using environmentalism as an example.

In chapter 10, I brought to bear Heidegger's critique of Western metaphysics upon the rise of ethical relativism. I contended that ethical relativism has been ubiquitous, for instance, in such modernist projects as positivism, as well as for postmodernists (which grew out of the perceived failure of modernism). I have developed one way to understand a Heideggerian contribution to ethics; one that is realist.

Though I do not go head-to-head with all the arguments that may be offered in favor of the ethical relativists, I outline a Heideggerian reply to two main ones. In a nutshell, I reject that ethical realism requires correspondence with mind-independent values (that are outside of the spacio-temporal world). An upshot of an emergent view, that is, that values arise in practices, is a salvo against the ethical relativist. We could say, adopting Heideggerian jargon, that values are neither purely subjective nor objective, but part of a life-world (*Lebsenwelt*). For Heidegger, the values that underlie ethics, are part of an entire orientation towards the world.

Second, I suggest that the fact of cultural difference does not necessitate the adoption of ethical relativism if we consider, for example, the circumstances in which abhorrent practices occurred. Moreover, we are not forced to value relativism. According to Heidegger, a certain life-world is preferable—one where we enjoy a fundamental relationship to being—which is the basis, I have argued, to avoid ethical relativism. If there is inevitability about the nature of our circumstance (as Heidegger thinks there is), we may also remain optimistic that we would, eventually, arrive at one ethic—the right one in terms of what we are meant to be. The moral realist finds a safe haven with Heidegger, which is fitting as he is one of the key exponents of romanticism of the twentieth century.

In chapter 10, I considered some current naturalistic arguments in favor of moral realism, and at least consistent with Heidegger's thought. I argued that Hume was only in part on the right track in thinking reason must be a slave to the passions.[1] Our passions are far from arbitrary but are the slow and arduous process of brain evolution in its commerce with organizational behavior and environment.

Also, I offered neuroethical reasons to buoy up Heidegger's reading of Kant. Providing the individual's rationale for action, there is mounting evidence that moral emotions are the sine qua non of such decision making. The amygdala has been identified as an older module of the brain, part of the limbic system, where emotions are processed. Providing the global rationale, primitive emotions relate to safeguarding our welfare in a social setting. Leaving its mark on brain ontogeny, we organize to survive in an environment, which shapes our emotional capacities and inclinations, too.

I have contended that the being-experience may be part of a rational reconstruction of ethical knowledge. Insofar, however, that the being-experience is part of ethical maturation, I conjectured, that it helps us understand the moral emotions and behavior we already engage in, thus, providing a rationale and reinforcing them. I suggested that the being-experience renders our lives—which are framed by the language of ethics—intelligible, which probably requires the PFC, and has emotional resonance in the amygdala.

I pointed out that Heidegger's account of the foundation of ethics may be of use to researchers who approach the problem from various angles. Heidegger may be able to offer an experientially rich descriptive account of the base of some ethical feelings (such as care and submission), useful to a sociobiologist, at the very least, offering a rational reconstruction of the foundation of ethics. Heidegger's ethical eschatology can rescue the sociobiologist from ethical relativism also.

In attempting to give a figure to the being-relationship, I have configured it as an experience. The consequent of the mystical experience of communing with being is to experience the consequences to thinking that

---

1. Hume, *Treatise on Human Nature*, 462. We may wonder at my introducing a term related to a specific passion, like "care" (*Sorge*), that was used by Heidegger in *Being and Time*. I refer to "care," however, to summarize what I have said. Suffice it to say that explaining Heidegger's analysis of the emotions goes beyond my purpose (and it has already been done in a number of commentaries on *Being and Time*).

Prospects for Moral Realism

the world is good. My investigation, then, has been to see to what extent a simple idea—that the world is good—could be the basis of an ethics. Here is a summary of my argument.

a. at the base of ethics are *values*.

b. values serve some *functions that are part of collective practices*.

c. *practices* arise in circumstances.

d. The circumstances in which we find ourselves are part and parcel of the unfolding of being. There is an *ethical eschatology* implicit in Heidegger's writings.

e. recognizing something like perhaps the goodness of the world—the way the world is unfolding—gives rise to *emotions*, often associated with care and submission, which are *consequent to having obtained a fundamental relationship to being*.

It would seem, however, that young children learn about ethical behavior before having entered into a fundamental relationship with being. They may not have a view about the goodness of the world one way or another. There are two points. First, a justification for ethics need not motivate every action. We may behave ethically out of habit or by commitment to a code of behavior. So-called ethical behavior may carry on out of force of habit without member practitioners having obtained a fundamental relationship to being. Yet we also may rightly wonder about the basis of the habit, custom, or code we adhere to.

Second, obtaining a fundamental relationship to being can still be deemed an ethical retrieval, insofar as it harkens us back to the very sentiments that motivated it in the first place. Though ethics may be learned by route, the practices that constitute it, must have began somewhere. Ethical practice, which we are, perhaps unwittingly, already inculcated in, finds justification in an orientation towards the world which is philosophically, though not necessarily anthropologically, consequent to having entered into a fundamental relationship to being.

The following caveats deserve mention. Developing a Heideggerian ethic often makes it difficult to work out the mechanisms. How do we get from a fundamental relationship to being to a specific ethic? Suffice it to note that I have attempted to demonstrate, in concrete terms, what a Heideggerian ethics would look like. I argued, by way of analogy, that a Heideggerian would be an environmental one. Vagueness, we may hope, is a boon, furthermore, if it provides the flexibility required to tailor specific moral principles to particular situations. My replies are optimistic, of course.

My purpose has been to develop, as far as I can, Heidegger's ethics as he envisioned it as first requiring a fundamental relationship to being. In so doing, I have tried to develop a view that is as plausible as I can. I have also wished to make plain what one has to buy into if one adopts the view I outline. Even if one does not go whole hog with Heidegger, there are still other things we have learned about moral realism along the way.

Heidegger has contributed to understanding the way we pose questions in ethics, both in terms of content and historically. Conviction about a Heideggerian ethic, I think, can only come if we find it more attractive than alternative accounts and consistent with our experience. The veracity of a Heideggerian ethic, unlike its validity, and like most philosophical theses, requires believing it.

So must we believe that a fundamental relationship is necessary for ethics? Unlikely. I have argued that a fundamental relationship to being can be conceived of as a mystical experience that supports proclivities we already have acquired genetically, ontogenetically, and potentially even epigenetically. The root of ethics lies in our evolutionary history coupled with our interpersonal experiences, especially when young, that take place in a socio-cultural context. At the very least, still, we could take Heidegger's style of ethics as an abstract garb to make sense of the ethical world we find ourselves in. I am unsure if a fundamental relationship to being is necessary for ethics. Some will inevitably find the idea of a fundamental relationship to being as underlying an ethics edifying. Others will not. In writing this book, we can rightly infer that I was attracted to the idea, even if having to concede that it may be superfluous.

I have two findings. First, Heidegger provided the basis to analyze, and criticize, moral relativism. In short, ethics tells us something about ourselves, who we are, not about mind-independent values. Also, in order to overcome the challenge of epistemic change, we can conceive of ethics, the right one, as the outcome of the unfolding of being expressed in an ideal socio-cultural manifestation. Both points I developed, in a unique way, taking into account some current naturalistic writings in ethics. Second, I suggested that an environmental philosophy is consistent with a Heideggerian ethics by looking to the writings of Schweitzer. We have at least one route to moral realism rooted in the tradition of Aristotle (Heidegger's analysis of Dasien) and German Idealism (his ethical eschatology), both of which are held together by the experience he seeks of being that is only perhaps possible at the beginning of history.

Much of Heidegger's efforts are attempts to understand ourselves, which I have extended to include, history, psychology, and neurology. In difference we find we are the same. We need to further study, using empirical and anecdotal methods, what we should be and try to achieve it, too. We are on a way that is bigger than ourselves.

Bibliography

Aiken, N. E. *The Biological Origins of Art.* Westport, CT: Praeger, 1998.
Anscombe, G. E. M. "Modern Moral Philosophy." *Philosophy* 33 (1958) 1–16.
Aquinas, Thomas. *Summa Theologica.* Translated by Fathers of the Dominican Province. London: Burns, Oates, and Washburne, 1927.
Aristotle. *Categories.* In *The Basic Works of Aristotle*, edited by R. McKeon, 7–37. New York: Random House, 1941.
———. *Metaphysics.* In *The Basic Works of Aristotle*, edited by R. McKeon, 381–926. New York: Random House, 1941.
———. *Physics.* In *The Basic Works of Aristotle*, edited by R. McKeon, 218–397. New York: Random House, 1941.
Armstrong, D. M. *Belief, Truth and Knowledge.* Cambridge: Cambridge: University Press, 1973.
Augustine. *The Confessions of St. Augustine.* Translated by E. B. Pusey. London: Everyman's Library, 1966.
Ayer, A. J. "Critique of Ethics and Theology." In *Essays on Moral Realism*, edited by G. Sayre-McCord, 27–40. Ithaca, NY: Cornell University Press, 1988.
Barsam, A. P. "Schweitzer, Jainism, and Reverence for Life." In *Reverence for Life: The Ethics of Albert Schweitzer for the Twenty-First Century*, edited by M. Myer and K. Bergel, 207–45. Syracuse: Syracuse University Press, 2002.
Benacerraf, P. "What Mathematical Truth Could Not Be—II." In *Sets and Proofs*, edited by S. B. Cooper and J. K. Truss, 27–52. London Mathematical Society Lecture Note Series 258. Cambridge: Cambridge: University Press, 2001.
Benjamin, A. "Time and Task, Benjamin and Heidegger Showing the Present." In *Walter Benjamin's Philosophy*, edited by A. Benjamin and P. Osborne, 216–50. New York: Routledge, 1994.
Bernasconi, R. "Heidegger's Destruction of Phronesis." *Southern Journal of Philosophy* 28 (1989) 127–47.
Berthoz, S., et al. "Affective Response to One's Own Moral Violations." *NeuroImage* 312 (2006) 945–50.
Block, N., ed. *Readings in Philosophical Psychology.* 2 vols. Cambridge, MA: Harvard University Press, 1980–81.
Bobrowski, J. *Shadowlands: Selected Poems.* Translated by R. Mead and M. Mead. New York: New Directions, 1984.
Boden, M. A. *Mind as Machine: A History of Cognitive Science.* 2 vols. Oxford: Oxford University Press, 2006.

Bibliography

Bond, G. J. *Reason and Value*. Cambridge: Cambridge University Press, 1983.
Boyd, R. "How to Be a Moral Realist." In *Essays on Moral Realism*, edited by G. Sayre-McCord, 181–228. Ithaca, NY: Cornell University Press, 1988.
———. "Materialism without Reductionism: What Physicalism Does Not Entail." In *Readings in Philosophical Psychology*, edited by N. Block, 1:67–106. Cambridge, MA: Harvard University Press, 1980.
Bradley, A. C. "Hegel's Theory of Tragedy." In *Hegel on Tragedy*, translated by A. Paolucci and H. Paolucci, 366–88. New York: Harper & Row, 1975.
Bratman, M. E. "Planning and Temptation." In *Mind and Morals: Essays on Cognitive Science and Ethics*, edited by M. L. Friedman and A. Clark, 293–310. Cambridge, MA: MIT Press, 1996.
Brentano, F. *The Foundation and Construction of Ethics*. Translated by E. Hughes. London: Routledge, 1973.
——— *The Origin of Our Knowledge of Right and Wrong*. Translated by M. Chisholm and H. Schneewind. New York: Routledge, 1969.
——— *The Several Senses of Being in Aristotle*. Translated by R. George. Berkeley: University of California Press, 1975.
Brook, A. *Kant and the Mind*. Cambridge: Cambridge University Press, 1994.
Brook, A., and K. Akins, eds. *Cognition and the Brain: The Philosophy and Neuroscience Movement*. Cambridge: Cambridge University Press, 2005.
Brook, A., and R. Stainton. *Knowledge and Mind*. Cambridge, MA: MIT Press, 2000.
Bruns, G. *Heidegger's Estrangements: Language, Truth, and Poetry in the Later Writings*. New Haven, CT: Yale University Press, 1998.
Bungay, S. *Beauty and Truth: A Study of Hegel's Aesthetics*. Oxford: Oxford University Press, 1984.
Bury, R. G., trans. and ed. *Plato*. Cambridge, MA: Harvard University Press.
Caputo, J. D. *Against Ethics*. Bloomington: Indiana University Press, 1993.
———. *Demythologizing Heidegger*. Bloomington: Indiana University Press, 1993.
———. "Disseminating Originary Ethics and the Ethics of Dissemination." In *The Question of the Other: Essays in Contemporary Continental Philosophy*, edited by A. B. Dallary and C. E. Scott, 55–62. Albany: State University of New York Press, 1989.
———. *Heidegger and Aquinas*. New York: Fordham University Press, 1982.
———. *The Mystical Element in Heidegger's Thought*. New York: Fordham University Press, 1986.
Casebeer, W. D. *Natural Ethical Facts: Evolution, Connectionism, and Moral Cognition*. Cambridge, MA: MIT Press, 2003.
Churchland, P. "The Neural Representation of the Social World." In *Mind and Morals: Essays on Cognitive Science and Ethics*, edited by M. L. Friedman and A. Clark, 99–173. Cambridge, MA: MIT Press, 1996.
Cooper, B., and J. K. Truss, eds. *Sets and Proofs*. London Mathematical Society Lecture Notes Series 258. Cambridge: Cambridge University Press, 1999.
Cooper, J. M., ed. *Complete Works of Plato*. Indianapolis: Hackett, 1997.
———. *Reason and Human Good in Aristotle*. Cambridge, MA: Harvard University Press, 1975.
Crisp, R., and M. Slote. *Virtue Ethics*. Oxford: Oxford University Press, 1997.
Deigh, J. "Empathy and Universalizability." In *Mind and Morals: Essays on Cognitive Science and Ethics*, edited by M. L. Friedman and A. Clark, 200–220. Cambridge, MA: MIT Press, 1996.

Dennett, D. C. *Darwin's Dangerous Idea: Evolution and the Meanings of Life*. New York: Touchstone, 1995.
Descartes, R. *Discourse on Method and Meditation on First Philosophy*. Translated by D. Cress. Indianapolis: Hackett, 1980.
———. *Passions of the Soul*. Translated by S. Voss. Indianapolis: Hackett, 1989.
Desmond, W. *Art and the Absolute: A Study of Hegel's Aesthetics*. Albany: State University of New York Press, 1986.
Doris, J. M. *Lack of Character*. New York: Cambridge University Press, 2002.
Doris, J. M., et al., eds. *The Moral Psychology Handbook*. Oxford: Oxford University Press, 2010.
Dostal, R. J. "Time and Phenomenology." In *The Cambridge Companion to Heidegger*, edited by C. Guignon, 120–48. Cambridge: Cambridge University Press, 1993.
Dreyfus, H. *Being-in-the-World: A Commentary on Heidegger's Being and Time*. Cambridge, MA: MIT Press, 1970.
Earman, J. J. "Till the End of Time." In *Foundations of Space-Time*, edited by J. J. Earman et al., 109–33. Minneapolis: University of Minnesota Press, 1977.
Edwards, P. *Heidegger's Confusions*. Amherst, NY: Prometheus, 2004.
Etter, B. K. *Between Transcendence and Historicism: The Ethical Nature of the Arts in Hegelian Aesthetics*. Albany: State University of New York Press, 2006.
Farías, V. *Heidegger and Nazism*. Edited by J. Margolis and T. Rockmore. Philadelphia: Temple University Press, 1989.
Feferman, S. *In the Light of Logic*. New York: Oxford University Press, 1998.
Finnis, J. M. *Natural Law and Natural Rights*. Oxford: Clarendon, 1980.
Flanagan, O. J. "Ethics Naturalized, Ethics as Human Ecology." In *Mind and Morals: Essays on Cognitive Science and Ethics*, edited by M. L. Friedman and A. Clark, 19–43. Cambridge, MA: MIT Press, 1996.
Frassen, B. van. "Against Naturalized Epistemology." In *On Quine: New Essays*, edited by P. Leonardi and M. Santambrogio, 68–88. Cambridge: Cambridge University Press, 1995.
Frege, G. *The Foundations of Arithmetic: A Logico-Mathematical Enquiry into the Concept of Number*. Translated by J. L. Austin. Oxford: Blackwell, 1953.
———. "Thoughts." In *Collected Papers on Mathematics, Logic, and Philosophy*, edited by B. McGuinness, 351–72. Translated by M. Black et al. Oxford: Blackwell, 1984.
Friedman, M. L., and A. Clark, eds. *Mind and Morals: Essays on Cognitive Science and Ethics*. Cambridge, MA: MIT Press, 1996.
Frings, M. S., ed. *Heidegger and the Quest for Truth*. Chicago: Quadrangle, 1968.
Gazzaniga, M. S. *The Ethical Brain*. New York: Dana, 2005.
Gibbs, N. "The EQ Factor." In *Annual Editions: Child Growth and Development*, edited by E. N. Junn and C. Boyatzis, 90–96. New York: McGraw-Hill, 1999–2000.
Gibson, R. "Quine on the Naturalizing of Epistemology." In *On Quine: New Essays*, edited by P. Leonardi and M. Santambrogio, 89–103. Cambridge: Cambridge University Press, 1995.
Gilson, E. *Being and Some Philosophers*. Toronto: Pontifical Institute for Medieval Studies, 1952.
Goldman, A. I. "Simulation and Interpersonal Utility." In *Mind and Morals: Essays on Cognitive Science and Ethics*, edited by M. L. Friedman and A. Clark, 181–98. Cambridge, MA: MIT Press, 1996.

Bibliography

Greene, J. D., et al. "The Neural Bases of Cognitive Conflict and Control in Moral Judgement." *Neuron* 44 (2004) 389-400.

Grieder, A. "What Did Heidegger Mean by 'Essence'?" *Journal of the British Society for Phenomenology* 19 (1988) 64-89.

Grube, G. M. A., trans. *Plato's Republic*. Indianapolis: Hackett, 1992.

Guignon, C., ed. *The Cambridge Companion to Heidegger*. Cambridge: Cambridge University Press, 1993.

———. *Heidegger and the Problem of Knowledge*. Indianapolis: Hackett, 1983.

Guyer, P. "Thought and Being: Hegel's Critique of Kant's Theoretical Philosophy." In *The Cambridge Companion to Hegel*, edited by F. C. Beiser, 177-210. Cambridge: Cambridge University Press, 1993.

Hacking, I. *Representing and Intervening*. Cambridge: Cambridge University Press, 1983.

Hahn, H. *Empiricism, Logic, and Mathematics*. Edited by Brian McGuinness. Boston: Reidel, 1980.

Haidt, J. "The Emotional Dog and Its Rational Tail: A Social Intuitionist Approach to Moral Judgement." *Psychological Review* 108 (2001) 814-34.

Halper, E. "The Logic of Art: Beauty and Nature." In *Hegel and Aesthetics*, edited by W. Maker, 187-202. Albany: State University of New York Press, 2000.

Hamburger. M., trans. *Freiedrich Hölderlin: Poems and Fragments*. Cambridge: Cambridge University Press, 1980.

Hauser, M. *Moral Minds: How Nature Designed Our Universal Sense of Right and Wrong*. New York: HarperCollins, 2006.

Hegel, G. W. F. *The Encyclopaedia Logic with the Zusätze*. Translated by T. F. Geratets et al. Indianapolis: Hackett, 1991.

———. *Faith and Knowledge*. Translated by W. Cerf and H. S. Harris. Albany: State University of New York Press, 1977.

———. *Natural Law*. Translated by T. M. Knox. Philadelphia: University of Pennsylvania Press, 1979.

———. *Philosophy of Right*. Translated by T. M. Knox. Oxford: Clarendon, 1942.

———. *System of Ethical Life*. Translated by H. S. Harris and T. M. Knox. Albany: State University of New York Press, 1975.

Heidegger, M. *Aristotle's Metaphysics [theta] 1-3*. Translated by W. Brogon and Peter Warnek. Bloomington: Indiana University Press, 1955.

———. *Basic Concepts*. Translated by G. E. Aylesworth. Bloomington: Indiana University Press, 1993.

———. *Basic Problems of Phenomenology*. Translated by A. Hofstadter. Bloomington: Indiana University Press, 1982.

———. *Being and Time*. Translated by J. Macquarrie and E. Robinson. New York: Harper & Row, 1962.

———. *The Concept of Time*. Translated by W. McNeill. Cambridge: Cambridge University Press, 1992.

———. *Discourse on Thinking*. Translated by J. M. Anderson and E. Hans Freund. New York: Harper & Row, 1966.

———. *Early Greek Thinking*. Translated by D. F. Krell and F. A. Capuzzi. New York: Harper & Row, 1975.

———*The Essence of Reasons*. Translated by T. Malick. Evanston, IL: Northwestern University Press, 1969.

———. *Existence and Being*. Chicago: Henry Regnery, 1949.

———. *Hegel's Concept of Experience*. Translated by J. G. Gray and F. D. Wieck. New York: Harper & Row, 1970.
———. *Hegel's Phenomenology of Spirit*. Translated by P. Emad and K. Maly. Bloomington: Indiana University Press, 1988.
———. *Heraclitus Seminar, 1966–67*. Translated by C. H. Seibert. Tuscaloosa: University of Alabama Press, 1979.
———. *History of the Concept of Time: Prologomena*. Translated by T. Kisiel. Bloomington: Indiana University Press, 1985.
———. *Holderin's Hymn "The Ister."* Translated by W. McNeill and J. Davis. Bloomington: Indiana University Press, 1995.
———. *Identity and Difference*. Translated by J. Stambaugh. New York: Harper & Row, 1969.
———. *An Introduction to Metaphysics*. Translated by R. Manheim. New York: Doubleday, 1960.
———. *Kant and the Problem of Metaphysics*. Translated by R. Taft. Bloomington: Indiana University Press, 1990.
———. "Letter on Humanism." In *Martin Heidegger: Basic Writings*, edited by D. F. Krell, 213–66. New York: HarperCollins, 1993.
———. *Metaphysical Foundations of Logic*. Translated by M. Heim. Bloomington: Indiana University Press, 1990.
———. *On the Way to Language*. Translated by D. Hertz and J. Stambaugh. New York: Harper & Row, 1971.
———. *On Time and Being*. Translated by J. Stambaugh. New York: Harper & Row.
———. "Only a God Can Save Us Now." Translated by M. P. Alter and J. D. Caputo. *Philosophy Today* 20 (1976) 267–85.
———. *Parmenides*. Translated by A. Schuwer and R. Rojcewicz. Bloomington: Indiana University Press, 1992.
———. *The Piety of Thinking*. Translated by J. G. Hart and J. C. Maraldo. Bloomington: Indiana University Press, 1976.
———. *Plato's Sophist*. Translated by R. Rojcewicz and A. Schuwer. Bloomington: Indiana University Press, 1997.
———. *Poetry, Language and Thought*. Translated by A. Hofstadter. New York: Harper & Row, 2013.
———. *The Principle of Reason*. Translated by R. Lilly. Bloomington: Indiana University Press, 1991.
———. *The Question Concerning Technology*. Translated by W. Lovitt. New York: Harper & Row, 1977.
———*The Question of Being*. Translated by W. Kluback and J. T. Wilde. New Haven, CT: College and University Press, 1958.
———. *Schelling's Treatise on the Essence of Human Freedom*. Translated by J. Stambaugh. Athens: Ohio University Press, 1985.
———. *What Is a Thing?* Translated by W. B. Barton Jr. and V. Deutsch. Chicago: Henry Regnery, 1968.
———. *What Is Called Thinking?* Translated by F. D. Wieck and G. Gray. New York: Harper & Row, 1968.
———. *What Is Philosophy?* Translated by W. Kluback and J. T. Wilde. New Haven, CT: College and University Press, 1958.

Bibliography

Hirschfeld, L. A., and S. A. Gelman, eds. *Mapping the Mind: Domain Specificity in Cognition and Culture*. Cambridge: Cambridge University Press, 1994.
Hodge, J. *Heidegger and Ethics*. New York: Routledge, 1995.
Hooker, B., ed. *Truth in Ethics*. Oxford: Blackwell, 1996.
Hoy, D. C., ed. *Foucault: A Critical Reader*. Oxford: Blackwell, 1986.
Hume, D. *Treatise on Human Nature*. New York: Oxford University Press, 2000.
Husserl, E. *The Phenomenology of Internal-Time Consciousness*. Edited by M. Heidegger. Translated by J. S. Churchill. Bloomington: Indiana University Press, 1966.
Janicaud, D., and Jean-Francois Mattéi. *Heidegger from Metaphysics to Thought*. Translated by Michael Gendre. Albany: State University of New York Press, 1995.
Joseph, H. W. B. *Essays in Ancient and Modern Philosophy*. New York: Books for Libraries, 1971.
———. *Some Problems of Ethics*. Oxford: Clarendon, 1931.
Kagan, J. *The Nature of the Child*. New York: Basic Books, 1984.
Kahn, C. H. "Why Existence Does Not Emerge as a Distinct Concept in Greek Philosophy." In *Philosophies of Existence Ancient and Medieval*, edited by P. Morewedge, 323–34. New York: Fordham University Press, 1982.
Kant, I. *Critique of Practical Reason*. Translated by L. W. Beck. Indianapolis: Bobbs-Merrill, 1958.
———. *Critique of Pure Reason*. Translated by N. K. Smith. London: Macmillan, 1989.
———. *Critique of the Power of Judgement*. Translated by P. Guyer and E. Matthews. Cambridge: Cambridge University Press, 2000.
———. *Foundations of the Metaphysics of Morals*. Edited by R. P. Wolff. Translated by L. W. Beck. Indianapolis: Bobbs-Merrill, 1969.
———. *Lectures on Ethics*. Translated by L. Field. New York: Harper & Row, 1963.
———. *The Metaphysical Elements of Justice*. Translated by J. Ladd. New York: Macmillan, 1985.
———. *The Metaphysical Principle of Virtue*. Translated by J. Ellington. Indianapolis: Bobbs-Merrill, 1964.
———. *The Metaphysics of Morals*. Translated by M. Gregor. Cambridge: Cambridge University Press, 1991.
———. *Observations on the Feeling of the Beautiful and Sublime*. Translated by J. T. Goldthwait. Berkeley: University of California Press, 1960.
Kenny, D. *Aquinas: A Collection of Critical Essays*. Garden City, NY: Anchor, 1969.
Kitcher, P. "Developmental Decomposition and the Future of Human Behavioural Ecology." *Philosophy of Science* 57 (1990) 96–117.
———. "The Evolution of Human Altruism." *The Journal of Philosophy* 90 (1993) 497–516.
———. *The Nature of Mathematical Knowledge*. Oxford: Oxford University Press, 1984.
———. "Psychological Altruism, Evolutionary Origins, and Moral Rules." *Philosophical Studies* 89 (1998) 283–316.
———. *Vaulting Ambition: Sociobiology and the Quest for Human Nature*. Cambridge, MA: MIT Press, 1985.
Knasas, J. F. X. "A Heideggerian Critique of Aquinas and a Gilsonian Reply." *Thomist* 58 (1994) 415–439.
Krell, D. F., ed. *Martin Heidegger: Basic Writings*. New York: HarperCollins, 1993.
Kunitz, S., ed. *The Essential Blake*. New York: Ecco, 1987.

Bibliography

Leonardi, P., and M. Santambrogio, eds. *On Quine: New Essays.* Cambridge: Cambridge University Press, 1995.

Livingstone, M. *Vision and Art: The Biology of Seeing.* New York: Abrams, 2002.

Lumsden, C. J., and E. O. Wilson. *Genes, Minds, and Culture: The Coevolutionary Process.* Cambridge, MA: Harvard University Press, 1981.

———. *Promethean Fire: Reflections on the Origin of Mind.* Cambridge, MA: Harvard University Press, 1983.

MacArthur, R. H., and E. O. Wilson. *The Theory of Island Biogeography.* Princeton, NJ: Princeton University Press 1967.

MacIntyre, A. *After Virtue.* 2nd ed. Notre Dame: University of Notre Dame Press, 1988.

———. *Whose Justice? Whose Rationality?* Notre Dame: University of Notre Dame Press, 1997.

Mackie, J. L. *The Cement of the Universe.* Oxford: Oxford University Press, 1974.

———. *Ethics: Inventing Right and Wrong.* New York: Penguin, 1977.

Macomber, W. B. *The Anatomy of Disillusion.* Evanston, IL: Northwestern University Press, 1967.

Malebranche, N. *Dialogues on Metaphysics and Religion.* Edited by N. Jolley. Translated by D. Scott. Cambridge: Cambridge University Press, 1992.

———. *The Search after Truth.* Translated by T. M. Lennon and P. J. Olscamp. Cambridge: Cambridge University Press, 1965.

Mandelstam, O. E. *The Complete Poetry of O. E. Mandelstam.* Translated by R. Raffel and A. Burago. Albany: State University of New York Press, 1973.

———. *The Voronezh Notebooks: Poems, 1935–1937.* Translated by R. McKane and E. McKane. Newcastle upon Tyne, UK: Bloodaxe, 1996.

Martin, M. W. "Rethinking Reverence for Life." In *Reverence for Life: The Ethics of Albert Schweitzer for the Twenty-First Century,* edited by M. Myer and K. Bergel, 204–13. Syracuse: Syracuse University Press, 2002.

Marx, Werner. *Heidegger and the Tradition.* Translated by T. Kisiel and M. Greene. Evanston, IL: Northwestern University Press, 1971.

Maslow, A. H. *Motivation and Personality.* New York: Harper, 1954.

———. *Toward a Psychology of Being.* Princeton, NJ: Van Nostrand, 1962.

Maslow, A. H., and B. Mittelmann. *Principles of Abnormal Psychology: The Dynamics of Psychic Illness.* New York: Harper, 1951.

McCormick, P. J. *Fictions, Philosophies, and the Problem of Poetics.* Ithaca, NY: Cornell University Press, 1988.

———. *Heidegger and the Language of the World.* Ottawa: University of Ottawa Press, 1976.

———. "Heidegger, Politics and the Philosophy of History." *Philosophical Studies* 27 (1980) 196–211.

———. *Modernity, Aesthetics, and the Bounds of Art.* Ithaca, NY: Cornell University Press, 1999.

McDowell, J. *Mind and World.* Cambridge, MA: Harvard University Press, 1984.

———. *Mind, Value, Reality.* Cambridge, MA: Harvard University Press, 1988.

———. "Values and Secondary Qualities." In *Essays on Moral Realism,* edited by G. Sayre-McCord, 166–80. Ithaca, NY: Cornell University Press, 1988.

McKeon, R., ed. and trans. *Basic Works of Aristotle.* New York: Random House, 1941.

McLellon, D., ed. *Marxism: The Essential Writings.* Oxford: Oxford University Press, 1988.

Bibliography

Mihalić, S. *Atlantis: Selected Poems, 1953–1983*. Translated by C. Simic and P. Kastmiler. Greenfield Center, NY: Greenfield Review, 1984.
Misak, C. J. *Truth and the End of Inquiry: A Peircean Account of Truth*. Oxford: Clarendon, 1991.
Moll, J., et al. "The Neural Basis of Human Moral Cognition." *Nature Reviews of Neuroscience* 6 (2005) 1–22. Doi: 10.1038/nrn1768.
Moore, G. E. *Principia Ethica*. Cambridge: Cambridge University Press, 1984.
Murdoch, I. *A Message to the Planet*. Toronto: Random House, 1989.
———. *The Sovereignty of the Good over Other Concepts*. London: Cambridge University Press, 1967.
Myer, M., and K. Bergel, eds. *Reverence for Life: The Ethics of Albert Schweitzer for the Twenty-First Century*. Syracuse: Syracuse University Press, 2002.
Nicholson, G. *Illustrations of Being: Drawing upon Metaphysics and Upon Heidegger*. Atlantic Highlands, NJ: Humanities, 1992.
Nielson, K. *Ethics without God*. London: Prometheus, 1973.
———. *God and the Grounding of Morality*. Ottawa: University of Ottawa Press, 1991.
O'Connor, D. J. *Aquinas and Natural Law*. London: Macmillan, 1967.
Olafson, F. A. *Heidegger and the Ground of Ethics*. Cambridge: Cambridge University Press, 1998.
Orr, R. *The Meaning of Transcendence*. Chico, CA: Scholars, 1981.
Oster, F., and E. O. Wilson. *Caste and Ecology in the Social Insects*. Princeton, NJ: Princeton University Press, 1978.
Ott, H. *Martin Heidegger: A Political Life*. Translated by A. Blunden. New York: Basic Books, 1983.
Outka, G. H. *Religion and Morality*. Edited by G. H. Outka and J. P. Reeder Jr. Garden City, NY: Anchor, 1973.
Owens, J. "The Doctrine of Being in Aristotle's Metaphysics—Revisited." In *Philosophies of Existence Ancient and Medieval*, edited by P. Morewedge, 33–59. New York: Fordham University Press, 1982.
Paolucci, H., trans. *Hegel, on the Arts: Selections from G. W. F. Hegel's Aesthetics or the Philosophy of Fine Art*. 2nd ed. Smyrna, DE: Bagehot Council, 2001.
Paolucci, A., and H. Paolucci, eds. *Hegel on Tragedy*. New York: Harper & Row, 1975.
Petzet, H. W. *Encounters and Dialogues with Martin Heidegger, 1929–1976*. Translated by P. Emand and K. Maly. Chicago: University of Chicago Press, 1993.
Piaget, J. *The Moral Judgement of the Child*. Translated by M. Gabuin. New York: Free Press, 1965.
Pillow, K. *Sublime Understanding: Aesthetic Reflection in Kant and Hegel*. Cambridge, MA: MIT Press, 2000.
Plotinus. *The Enneads*. Edited by B. S. Page. Translated by S. MacKenna. 3rd rev. ed. London: Faber and Faber, 1962.
Prado, C. G. *Descartes and Foucault*. Ottawa: Ottawa University Press, 1992.
Premack, D., and A. J. Premack. "Moral Belief: Form vs. Content." In *Mapping the Mind: Domain Specificity in Cognition and Culture*, edited by L. A. Hirschfeld and S. A. Gelman, 149–68. Cambridge: Cambridge University Press, 1994.
Putnam, H. "Mathematical Necessity Reconsidered." In *On Quine: New Essays*, edited by P. Leonardi and M. Santambrogio, 267–82. Cambridge: Cambridge University Press, 1995.

———. *Mathematics, Matter, Method*. His Philosophical Papers 1. Cambridge: Cambridge University Press, 1979.
Quine, W. V. *From a Logical Point of View*. Cambridge, MA: Harvard University Press, 1953.
———. *Ontological Relativity*. New York: Columbia University Press, 1969.
———. *The Roots of Reference*. LaSalle, IL: Open Court, 1973.
———. *Word and Object*. Cambridge, MA: MIT Press, 1960.
Quinn, P. *Divine Commands and Moral Requirements*. Oxford: Clarendon, 1978.
Rabinow, P., and W. Sullivan, eds. *Interpretive Social Science: A Second Look*. Berkeley: University of California Press, 1987.
Railton, P. "Moral Realism." *The Philosophical Review* 9 (1986) 163–207.
Reichenbach, H. *Experience and Prediction*. Chicago: University of Chicago Press, 1938.
Rescher, N. *Ethical Idealism*. Berkeley: University of California Press, 1987.
Richardson, W. "Heidegger and Aristotle." *Heythrop Journal* 5 (1964) 58–64.
———. *Heidegger: Through Phenomenology to Thought*. The Hague: Nijhoff, 1963.
Rilke, R. M. *Selected Works*. Vol. 2. Translated by J. B. Leishman. New York: New Directions, 1967.
Rockmore, T. *On Heidegger's Nazism and Philosophy*. Berkeley: University of California Press, 1992.
Rorty, R. *Consequences of Pragmatism*. Minneapolis: University of Minnesota Press, 1982.
———. *Contingency, Irony, and Solidarity*. Cambridge: Cambridge University Press, 1989.
———. *Essays on Heidegger and Others*. Cambridge: Cambridge University Press, 1991.
Rose, D. *Consciousness: Philosophical, Psychological, and Neural Theories*. Oxford: Oxford University Press, 2006.
Rose, F. C. "The Neurology of Art: An Overview." In *Neurology of the Arts: Painting, Music, Literature*, edited by F. C. Rose, 43–76. London: Imperial College Press, 2004.
Safranski, R. *Martin Heidegger: Between Good and Evil*. Translated by E. Osers. Cambridge, MA: Harvard University Press, 1998.
Sayre-McCord, G., ed. *Essays on Moral Realism*. Ithaca, NY: Cornell University Press, 1988.
Schalow, F. *Imagination and Existence: Heidegger's Revival of the Kantian Ethic*. Lanham, MD: University Press of America, 1986.
Scheler, M. *Formalism in Ethics and a Non-formal Ethics of Value*. Evanston, IL: Northwestern University Press, 1973.
Scheman, N. "Feeling Our Way towards Moral Objectivity." In *Mind and Morals: Essays on Cognitive Science and Ethics*, edited by M. L. Friedman and A. Clark, 221–36. Cambridge MA: MIT Press, 1996.
Schweitzer, A. *The Light Within Us*. Westport, CT: Greenwood, 1971.
———. *Out of My Life and Thought: An Autobiography*. Translated by C. T. Campion. New York: Holt, 1973.
———. *The Philosophy of Civilization*. Translated by C. T. Campion. Tallahassee: University Press of Florida, 1981.
———. *Reverence for Life*. Translated by R. H. Fuller. New York: Harper & Row, 1966.
Searle, J. "How to Derive 'Ought' from 'Is.'" *The Philosophical Review* 73 (1964) 43–58.
Seidel, G. J. M. *Heidegger and the Pre-Socratics*. Lincoln: University of Nebraska Press, 1982.
Sellars, W. *Empiricism and the Philosophy of Mind*. Cambridge, MA: Harvard University Press, 1997.

Shapiro, J. B. "Heidegger: Virtue Is Knowledge." *Philosophy Today* 38 (1994) 400–418.
Shapiro, S. *Foundations without Foundationalism: A Case for Second-Order Logic*. Oxford: Oxford University Press, 1991.
Sikka, S. *Forms of Transcendence: Heidegger and Mystical Medieval Theology*. Albany: State University of New York Press, 1997.
Singer, P. *The Expanding Circle: Ethics and Socio-Biology*. New York: Farrar, Straus and Giroux, 1981.
———. *Hegel*. Oxford: Oxford University Press, 1983.
———. *Practical Ethics*. Cambridge: Cambridge University Press, 1993.
———. "The Triviality of the Debate over 'Is-Ought' and the Definition of 'Moral.'" *American Philosophical Quarterly* 10 (1973) 51–56.
Solso, R. L. *Cognition and the Visual Arts*. Cambridge, MA: MIT Press, 1994.
———. "The Cognitive Neuroscience of Art: A Preliminary fMRI Observation." *Journal of Consciousness Studies* 78 (2000) 75–85.
———. *The Psychology of Art and the Evolution of the Conscious Brain*. Cambridge, MA: MIT Press, 2005.
Spengler, O. *The Decline of the West*. 2 vols. Translated by C. F. Atkinson. 1918. Reprint, New York: Knopf, 1973.
Spinoza, B. *Ethics*. Translated by G. H. R. Parkinson. Oxford: Oxford University Press, 2000.
Stambaugh, J. *The Finitude of Being*. Albany: State University of New York Press, 1992.
———. *Thoughts on Heidegger*. Washington, DC: University Press of America, 1986.
Stevenson, C. L. *Ethics and Language*. New Haven, CT: Yale University Press, 1944.
Sumner, W. G. *Folkways*. New York: Dover, 1940.
Thoreau, H. D. *Walden and Civil Disobedience*. New York: Penguin, 1986.
Tietz, J. "Heidegger on Realism and the Correspondence Theory of Truth." *Dialogue* 32 1 (1993) 59–76.
Urmson, J. O. *The Emotive Theory of Ethics*. London: Hutchinson, 1968.
Vail, L. M. *Heidegger and Ontological Difference*. University Park: Pennsylvania State University Press, 1972.
Vogel, L. *The Fragile "We": Ethical Implications of Heidegger's Being and Time*. Evanston, IL: Northwestern University Press, 1994.
Wicks, R. "Hegel's Aesthetics: An Overview." In *The Cambridge Companion to Hegel*, edited by F. C. Beiser, 348–77. Cambridge: Cambridge University Press, 1993.
Wiggins, D. *Needs, Values, Truth: Essays in the Philosophy of Value*. Oxford: Blackwell, 1987.
Williams, B. *Ethics and the Limits of Philosophy*. Cambridge, MA: Harvard University Press, 1985.
Williamson, R. K. *Introduction to Hegel's Philosophy of Religion*. Albany: State University of New York Press, 1984.
Wilson, E. O. *Biophilia*. Cambridge, MA: Harvard University Press, 1984.
———. *The Diversity of Life*. Cambridge, MA: Harvard University Press, 1992.
———. *The Insect Societies*. Cambridge, MA: Harvard University Press, 1971.
———. *The Moral Sense*. New York: Free Press, 1993.
———. *On Human Nature*. Cambridge, MA: Harvard University Press, 1978.
———. *Sociobiology: The New Synthesis*. Cambridge, MA: Harvard University Press, 1975.

Wilson, E. O., and W. H. Bossert. *A Primer of Population Biology*. Stamford, CT: Sinauer, 1971.

Winograd, T., and F. Flores. *Understanding Computers and Cognition: A New Foundation for Design*. Reading, MA: Addison-Wesley, 1987.

Wolin, R. *The Heidegger Controversy: A Critical Reader*. Cambridge, MA: MIT Press, 1993.

Wood, D. *The Deconstruction of Time*. Atlantic Highlands, NJ: Humanities, 1991.

Wright, G. H. von. *The Varieties of Goodness*. London: Routledge, 1963.

Wright, K. "Babies, Bonds and Brains." In *Annual Editions: Child Growth and Development*, edited by E. N. Junn and C. J. Boyatzis, 84–88. New York: McGraw-Hill, 2000.

Zaidel, D. *Neuropsychology of Art: Neurological, Cognitive and Evolutionary Perspectives*. New York: Psychology Press, 2005.

Zeki, S. *Inner Visions: An Exploration of Art and the Brain*. Oxford: Oxford University Press, 1999.

———. "Neural Concept Formation in Art: Dante, Michelangelo, Wagner." In *Neurology of the Arts: Painting, Music, Literature*, edited by F. C. Rose, 13–42. London: Imperial College Press, 2004.

———. *A Vision of the Brain*. Oxford: Blackwell Scientific, 1993.

Index

"About Abhorrence and Delight" (Descartes), 83
above time, 10
absolute, the, knowing, 88, 90
absolute idea, 89
abstract citizens, 77
abstract concepts, 14
abstract moral reasoning, 118
aesthetic appreciation, 86
aesthetic realism, 86
aesthetic relativism, 86
aesthetics, Hegel's, 87, 143
agnosticism, 138
agrarian society, in the Old Testament, 103
agriculture, comparison with gas chambers, 35
akrasia, knowing the good and not doing it, 117
altruism, as self-destructive behavior, 137n120
ambiguity
   between emotion and reason, 129
   in Heidegger's writings, 16–17, 46
   towards mysticism, 99
amygdala, 120
   as a crucial part of neural circuitry, 123
   evaluation of one's social transgression, 122
   identified as an older module of the brain, 144
   learning socially appropriate behavior, 123
   linked to social relations and our welfare, 130
analytic ethics, 24
anarchists, 34
ancestral language, loss of, 39
anger, causing release of catecholamines, 120
animal rights movement, differences between Schweitzer and, 103
anti-Semitism, Heidegger and, 33
appearance, as the truth of being, 88
apprehending being, 45
Aquinas, principles of natural law, 111
Arendt, Hannah, 33
Aristotle
   attempting ontology by way of first causes, 68
   criticisms of, 60
   dealing with ontical truths, 60
   defined ontology as a distinct science, 67
   ethics as personal, 105, 111
   four causes, 57
   not considering being but beings, 58
   ontology and, 57
   philosophy as the science of being, 4n18
   pleasure as awareness of an activity, 117

Index

Aristotle *(continued)*
   time linked to motion and change, 50
arithmetic, 135
art
   allowing us to access truth, 143
   connection to truth, 89
   evaluation of, 20
   as an expression of truth, 91
   goal of, for Hegel, 88
   mediation on works of, 19
   providing absolute truths, 91
   as a psychological affair, 91
   removed from matters of truth, 86
   within the scope of rational thought for Kant, 85
   as subjective for both Descartes and Spinoza, 86
   subjectivity of, 82–87
Art and the Absolute (Desmond), 90
articulation, of being, 11
Augustine, 50, 51
Austrian movement, of Christian Socialism, 31
autonomy, appearing only with reciprocity, 79

basic needs, according to Maslow, 44–45
Basic Problems of Phenomenology, 13, 25
basic values, underlying human conduct, 111
beautiful, property of being, 87
beauty
   about discovery without justification, 90
   based on mechanical reactions, 82
   dealing with "quality," 85
   as an intrinsic characteristic of an object, 90
beauty and truth, Hegel's connection of, 87
Beauty and Truth: A Study of Hegel's Aesthetics (Bungay), 87
the "because"
   is without "why," 64
   pointing to the essence of being, 64
   of the rose, 68
   suggesting a reason for the blooming of the rose, 65
   as universal, 69
beginning (*Angung*), outlasting everything, 32
behaviors
   helping us avoid pain, 108
   shaping biological profile of organisms, 133–34
Being. *See also* beings
   bestowing itself to us in beings, 63
   can never first have a ground/reason, 63
   as the general characteristics of particular beings, 58
   rupture in our relationship to, 91
being
   as abstract, 58
   as the beginning, 12
   co-dependent with beings, 65
   connection with time, 10
   consequences of forgetting of, 15
   construed as a thing, 14
   disclosedness of making possible beings, 59
   distinguishing from particular beings, 13
   estranged from, 12
   forgetfulness of by many philosophers, 57
   fundamental relationship with, 11
   as ground/reason, 64
   Heidegger's story of, 40–41
   how not to relate to, 9
   identified with history, 42
   including four problems, 11
   interpreting by the way of time, 13
   kinship with reason, 62

Index

manifest in the history of the world, 17
not having a reason, 64
not the same as nature, 37
as origin of the history of the West, 9
out of sync with, 12
particularizing itself in individual things, 68
path to, 64
relationship to as lost, 14
seeking a union with, 17
as that which is most general posing a problem, 58
as a theoretical and objective matter, 15
in touch with, 19
understanding through time, 29
as unique, 67
withdrawal of, 14
being and reason
belonging "together," 64
discussing in one breath, 63
ringing out in unison, 68
Being and Time
analysis of Dasein, 49
in no sense reading National Socialism into, 33
scant attention to the being-question, 1
being free, synonymous with behaving ethically, 26
being that is-there, how time is possible for, 53
Being-cognition, 45, 142
being-experience, 129, 144
being-in-the-world, 46, 55
being/nature, fundamental relationship with, 102
being-question (*Seinsfrage*)
answering requiring mysticism, 57
as the fundamental question of philosophy, 4
Heidegger's attempts to pursue, 10
being-relationship (*Bezug zum Seyn*)
as the basis of an ethics, 2, 49, 141
giving a figure to, 144
as a meta-cognitive experience, 130
psychology of, 43–46
beings. *See also* Being; being
always individually occurring beings, 67
being completely divorced from, 67
consequent to an interpretation of being, 68
"being-with-one-another," 26
Between Transcendence and Historicism: The Ethical Nature of the Arts in Hegel's Aesthetics (Etter), 90
Bible, distinction between clean and unclean, 119
biological evidence, 136
biological genealogy, 137
biological responses, to moral dilemmas, 118
biology, determining possible behaviors, 133
Black Forest, 40
blooming, 62, 63
Boelen, B. J., 23
bonding requirements, 126
brain
evolution, 128
in the first months of life, 115
functioning, 120
malleability, and adaptability of, 125
ontogeny, 117
restructuring of ages of nine to eleven, 126
brain-based philosophy of life, 117
"Brains, Bonds, and Babies" (Wright), 125
Broad, C. D., 36

calculative thinking, 18
capacity, to be imprinted with knowledge, 117
"care" (*Sorge*), 144n1
caregiver, absence of, 124

Index

The Castle (Kafka), 105
causality, reason equating with, 61
causes, 68
chasm
    between finite and infinite, 10
    between ourselves and God, 90
    between particulars and universals, 143
child and primitive, respecting authority, 79
childhood, looked to for understanding behavior, 115
children
    morality development in, 126
    sensitivity to cues from parents, 125
    societies organized around kinship and, 119
    as tactile creatures, 104
Chinese Taoism, 23
Christian Socialist movement, 32
church, undermining authentic spirituality, 96
civilization, 93, 94
clock, 50, 53
clock-time, 52
coercion (unilateral respect), 79
cognition, faculty of, 85
cognitive access, 10, 17
cognitive and emotional processes, 121
cognitive competence, 125
cognitive control, 121
collective *telos*, 26
"collision of forces," in a tragedy, 89
concepts, ethics derived *a priori* from, 74
conscience, yielding, 130
Conservative Unionist view, 116
context. *See also* social context
    in which competencies are activated, 125
contextual social knowledge, 122
contradictions, in Heidegger's work, 35
cooperation, as the basis of mature morals, 79n46

correspondence theory of truth, 15
creative children, delighting in novel ideas, 125
criticism, not superseding experiences, 113
Critique of Practical Reason (Kant), 84
Critique of Pure Reason (Kant), 84
Critique of the Power of Judgement (Kant), 82, 84
culture, without freedom as tyranny, 23

darkening, 19
Dasein
    analytic of, 26–27, 130
    in Heidegger's later works, 5, 102
    reckoning with time, 51
    socio-cultural aspect of, 131–140
    as time, 53–56
    as transcendental ground of ontological difference, 59
date, giving to the dateable, 52
death
    Heidegger's claims about, 37–38
    in radically finite ways, 28
death camps, agony of, 20
decline, in a state of, 43
Decline of the West (Spengler), 42
deficiency-needs-cognition, 45
Der Ister (the Danube), Heidegger analyzed, 40
Descartes, 36, 82–83
desire
    according to Descartes, 83
    faculty of, 85
    generated by discovery of value, 112
destiny (*Geshik*)
    of being, 13–14, 17, 64
    notion of, 43
"destitute time," poet of a, 20
difference, between Being and being (ontological difference), 60
dignity
    in conjunction with the will, 74
    in unity with service, 26

disclosedness of Being, 59
discovery, playing no role in justification, 135
"distance," Heideggerian predicament and, 69
distinction, between creatures and their Creator, 66
drama, Hegel's account of, 89
duty
  determined by the Kantian thought experiment, 75
  entailing accordance with the highest good, 76
  leading to the highest good, 75
  never as pure as Kant made it out to be, 80
  as our ethical motivation, 77
duty and inclination, Kant's distinction between, 27
dying alone, Heidegger's claim about, 37

early writings, Heidegger's, 49
Earman, J. J., 54
Eckhart, Meister, 22
ecological behaviorism, 131
egoism, 34–35
Eliminative Unionist view, 116
emancipation, from the present, 14
emendations, responding to problems, 137
emergent view, upshot of, 143
emotional communication, nonverbal, 120
"The Emotional Dog and Its Rational Tail: A Social Intuitionist Approach to Moral Judgement" (Haidt), 120
emotional intelligence, 119
emotional life, growing out of the limbic system, 120
emotions
  goodness of the world giving rise to, 145
  indispensible in appreciation of the arts, 82
  informing moral judgements, 127
  never eradicated, 121
  not banned, 130
  playing a role in moral reasoning, 129
  reflecting the appraisal of value, 123
  relating to an entire socio-cultural world, 127
The Emotive Theory of Ethics (Urmson), 108
emotivism, rejecting, 113
emotivists, 107
"Empathy and Universalizability" (Deigh), 127
The Encyclopaedia Logic (Hegel), 88
end of history, Hegel providing the clue to, 143
Enlightenment, 32
entities, ability of feeling pleasure and pain, 103
environmental philosophy, 102, 146
environmentalism, 101–4
epigenetic effects, 133
epistemic change, 146
epistemic content, beginning with, 135
epistemology, as symptomatic of a malady, 15
"The EQ Factor" (Gibbs), 119
equalitarian justice, 79
essence
  of being, 64
  reason and, 65–70
  relationship with appearance, 88
essence/existence distinction, 66
eternal realm, giving birth to a temporal one, 50
ethic of Love, widened to universality, 96
ethical behavior, out of force of habit, 145
ethical concepts, as pseudoconcepts, 107

Index

ethical disputes, as conflicting attitudes, 107
ethical eschatology
   being optimistic about, 138
   in German idealism, 113
   implicit in Heidegger's writings, 145
   rescuing the sociobiologist from ethical relativism, 144
ethical experience, 78
ethical feelings, 144
ethical fundamentals, 110, 134
ethical ideal, of Schweitzer, 96
ethical impulses, neural basis of, 119
ethical judgements, universality of, 27, 110–11, 113
ethical knowledge, 81, 106
ethical mysticism, 98, 113
ethical naturalism, Heidegger and, 115–40
ethical norms, 128
ethical orientation, towards the world, 102
ethical point of view, 78
ethical problems, Heidegger giving no specific advice, 23
ethical reasoning, based upon values rooted in emotions, 129
ethical relations, Kant offering certain structural or formal features of, 77
ethical relativism
   arguments for, 106
   avoiding, 115, 139
   being skeptical of, 113
   consequence of a false dilemma, 106
   contemporary case for, 109–10
   defined, 132
   ethical change and rejection of a *telos* of history leading to, 109
   Heideggerian rebuttal of, 106–14
   looming large with the rise of anthropology, 128
   ubiquitous in modernist projects, 143
ethical sensibilities, emotional components to, 119
ethical view of life, inability to defend, 94
ethical words, 107
ethicists, disenchanted with prospects for moral realism, 2–3
ethics
   about human nature, 26
   about right and wrong, 83
   actualized by human freedom, 76–77
   arising when original thinking ends, 21
   based on appreciation of human nature, 138
   basing on a scientific understanding of human nature, 46
   basis of, 95
   built into our brains, 118
   cannot rest on metaphysics, 74
   closer to us than being, 4
   determined by our relationship to being, 141
   extending Heidegger's thought on, 22
   founded on a relationship to being (*Bezug zum Seyn*), 1
   founding on an attitude, 100
   grounding in the world, 27
   Heideggerian, 21–24
   leaving to society, 97
   letting beings be, 23
   modern accounts of, 30
   motivation in a mystical experience, 100
   originating in mysticism, 96
   in part accounted for biologically, 134
   preceding metaphysics, 5
   requiring a fundamental relationship to Being, 92, 146
   root of in our evolutionary history, 146
   Schweitzer's, 93–105

springing from the meeting of needs, 46
transmitted through stories, 46
Ethics (Spinoza), 82
Ethics and Language (Stevenson), 107
Ethics and the Limits of Philosophy (Williams), 77
Ethics: Inventing Right and Wrong (Mackie), 107
event knowledge, in the prefrontal cortex (PFC), 122
events
 of history, 42
 traced to spiritual causes, 94
everyday, as sense data of the British empiricists, 142
evolution
 of the brain, 128
 broadly defined, 132n99
 clarifying induction, 132
evolutionary theory, 139
existence
 as appearance, 88
 origin of the notion of, 66
experience of being, seeking, 143
experience-dependent pruning, 115
experience-expectant pruning, 115
experiences
 informing what we think reasonable, 113
 meaning to the individual, 45
"external object," 84

Fact and Value (Bond), 112
faith, 90
fallenness, 69
fascism, of Heidegger, 34
fate, mingling with tragedy, 41
"a figure of fun," Heidegger as, 38
"final end," organization aimed towards, 89
final solution, Heidegger and, 33
fine arts, beauty of, 88
finite, chasm with the infinite, 10

finite beings
 grasping being, 11
 knowing about, 58
finitude, as experience of an eternal presence, 28
first causes, 68
flexibility, as humans' evolutionary advantage, 134
"folkways," 108–9
forgetting of being, marking the "decline of the West," 19
"for-us," truth as, 15–16
foundation of ethics, Heidegger's account of, 144
foundational, resting on doctrinal, 135
foundational epistemology, 134
frame, beliefs resistant to change, 124
freedom
 arising from a will, 27
 as a particular sort of entity, 27
 providing the spectre of, 11
 required to have a pure will, 76
 without culture as barbarism, 23
fundamental ontology, 2
fundamental relationship to being, 13
 necessary for ethics, 146
 obtaining, 145
 retrieving, 16, 17
future, part of the destiny of being, 20

Gelassenheit, as "openness to the mystery," 22–23
genes, 132, 133
Genesis, eviction from the garden of Eden, 81
genetic mechanisms, influencing human behavior, 132
geopolitical environment, becoming a psychological environment, 44
German folk (*Volk*), realization of, 33
German Idealism, tradition of, 13
German nationalism, Heidegger seriously committed to, 34
German spirit (*Deutch-Geist*), 34

Index

global reasons, 129
God
    assuming the existence of, 75
    guaranteeing one's eternal reward, 76
    as the only holy, blessed, wise being, 76
    as "a regulative principle for our actions" for Kant, 85
God postulate, necessary for morality, 76
good
    conceptions of so lifeless, 94
    discouraging scientific investigation of, 139
    as the form of common life, 112
    linking to desire, 112
    as a non-natural property, 116
good and bad, knowledge of, 84
goodness, 113, 116
gratitude, as a mysterious law of existence, 97
Greek Tragedies, 88
Greenpeace, 102
ground of Dasein, relationship to, 70
ground of ethics, 23
grounding reason, 112
ground/reason
    as being, 64
    missing from being, 63
guilt, 123

Hegel, G. W. F., 36, 82
    absolute versus attention to history, 89
    aesthetics of, 82–92
    art as a vehicle to truth, 91
    art overcoming distinction between "I" and "God," 90
    on beauty, 92
    idealism or relativism, 87–91
    legacy of, 91–92
    on particular and universal, 87, 143
    unifying concerns of rationalists and empiricists, 88

Heidegger
    aggrandized history, 43
    blurring distinction between motivation and justification, 80
    building an ethics from his reading of Kant, 73
    calling into question separation of metaphysics from arts and ethics, 92
    critique of history of Western philosophy applied to ethics, 141
    earlier and later work of, 3
    ethical naturalism and, 115–140
    interpreting Kantian kingdom of ends, 80
    not anti-Semitic in the Nazi sense, 33
    perceived a fall from grace, 81
    posing questions in ethics, 146
    provided basis to analyze and criticize moral relativism, 146
    putting the being-question at the forefront, 111
    reading as a mystic, 69
    reading as a pantheist or panentheist, 70
    reflection of a poem, 62
    rejected Nazism, 34
    remedying complaints with Kant's ethics, 142
    rereading of Kant gaining neurological support, 130
    separating his philosophy from his politics, 142
    supported repudiation of The Treaty of Versailles, withdrawal from the League of Nations, and annexation of lands, 33
    thought Nazism opposed to technology, 33
Heidegger and Nazism (Farías), 31
Heideggerian doctrine, emptiness of, 37
Heideggerian ethic

buttressing environmentalism, 105
elucidating by allusions to Schweitzer, 93
as an orientation towards the world, 18
yesterday and, 1–5
yielding an orientation towards the world, 80
Heideggerian mystical ethics, 101
Heidegger's Confusions (Edwards), 36
Heraclitus, Heidegger's reading of, 11, 17
hereafter, as an object of faith, 28
"the hermeneutic circle," idea of, 109
Hierarchy of Needs, Maslow's, 44
higher needs, from later evolutionary development, 45
higher-order gratification, experiencing, 45
highest good, 75, 80
hints, remaining hints, 67n60
historical change, without eschatology, 110
historical role, of art, 88
historical time, 28
history
  having a moral end, 109
  realist view of, 12
  unfolding of, 91
  venture of predetermining, 42
Hölderlin
  glimpse of renewal, 39–40
  poetry of, 20
  tragedy flowing through the writings of, 42
"holocaust," failing to grasp the meaning of, 35
homeland (*Heimat*), desire for, 32
homelessness
  as being abandoned spiritually, 20
  in the world, 12
homeostatic property cluster, 116
human existence, as meaningful, 80

human freedom, not opposed to nature, 27
human history, darker side of, 41
human infants, unconcerned about fairness, 120
human nature, truths about, 3
human understanding, facilitated by pre-understandings, 109
human values, having a descriptive naturalistic science of, 45
humanisms, 21, 30
Hume, David, 129, 131
Husserl, treatment of time, 51

idealism, tension with realism, 87
idealist tendencies, Heidegger's own German, 92
Idealists, taking up the idea of a fall from grace, 81
ideas
  history of, 29
  as seemingly nowhere, 10
identification, between the eternal and temporal, 88
imagination, 11
impersonal moral dilemma, 120
Indian mysticism, ethical consequences of, 99
Indian philosophies, 98, 100
Indian sources, for Schweitzer's thought, 98
individual ethical acts, relationships with social context, 130
inductive argument, 106, 108
industrialized world, in the late twentieth century, 103
inferences, based on movement, 119
infinite, covering up primordial time, 53
innate dispositions, 124, 128
insect and vertebrate societies, similarities between, 132
instant (*Augenblick*), 29

Index

intrinsic value
  idea of, 102
  of nature, 103
  of properties of an object, 107
intuition, 120, 139
ironic philosophers, 110
is, as closer approximations of the *ought*, 139
is and *ought*, relationship between configured, 138
is includes *ought*, as a slogan, 139
is-ought problem
  arising, 134
  identified by David Hume, 131
  naturalized epistemological solving, 132
  paths to disarm, 140
  responding to, 135

Jainism, 98
Joseph, H. W. B., 112
Judeo-Christian thought, 102
justice, depends on free consent, 79
justification, divorced from discovery, 134–35

Kagan, Jerome, 123–25
Kant, 36
  on aesthetics and ethics, 86
  back to before, 25–30
  basis of ethics, 95
  on beauty, 90
  calling into question power of reason, 84–85
  conundrum of, 78
  deemed being as vacuous, empty and indeterminate, 58
  discerning the basis of morality, 74
  drawing a wall between what justifies ethics and what motivates it, 141–42
  ethical theory of, 76
  ethics about our relations with others, 105
  ethics of, 25–27
  grand theory of, 73–77
  Heidegger's appropriation of, 81
  Heidegger's reading of, 5, 81, 141
  highest good, 75
  ideal (to ban emotion from moral judgement) as not achievable, 117
  impressed by both scientific knowledge and moral knowledge, 77
  justification of ethics, 73
  knowledge limited by faculties of the mind, 86
  placed art within the intersubjective realm, 91
  providing putative claim of the subjectivity of the arts, 84
  pure practical reason leads to religion, 75
  rational reconstruction of ethics, 128
  remaining within the sensible world, 29
  setting the basis for an anthropology, 26
  thoughts compared to Hegel, 88
  what ought to be, 73
  will giving us dignity, 20
Kantain ethics, motivational feeling of, 81
Kantian, "rationalist" approach, 122
Kantian kingdom of ends, 26
Kantian thought experiment, 75
Kantians, trying to formalize the practice of ethics, 30
Kant's ethical program, Heidegger's reading of, 25
kingdom of ends, Kant's, 80
"knowing and feeling," fused after fourteen months, 119
knowledge, 109

language, mystical type of, 29
language philosophers, 38
Lao-Tzu, philosophy of, 95
League of Nations, withdrawal from, 33

INDEX

learning
  about the brain, 117
  occurs in the synapse, 118 n22
Leibniz, 60, 61
"Letter on Humanism," 20, 70
letting beings be
  declaration of, 23
  as negative, 101
  saying something about, 81
letting things be, as hopelessly vague, 24
letting-be, notion of, 22
"life problems," solving, 43
life-denial, Schweitzer avoiding, 99
life-world (*Lebsenwelt*), 143
linguistic turn, originator of, 91
literature, blurring of various forms of, 46
logos, 14
London cab drivers, special memory of, 116
love, as pleasure accompanied by the idea of an "external object," 84
love and hatred, related to usefulness and harm, 83
loving, ethic of, 23
lower-order needs, meeting first, 45

man, as shepherd of being, 21
Mandelstam, O. E., 20, 41–42
Marcuse, Herbert, 35
Maslow, 43–46
Maslow's Hierarchy of Needs, 44
material advancement, withdrawal of being and, 99
meaning of Being, 49
mechanisms, of Heideggerian ethic, 145
mechanization, of life and death, 35–36
mediation, on works of art, 19
meta-ethics, current predicament of, 3
metaphysical commitments, entailing ethical consequences, 49
metaphysical ethics
  Heidegger never intended, 22
  Schweitzer's, 143
metaphysical reflection, Heidegger's attitude towards, 16
metaphysics
  antipathy towards, 2n6
  as first ground of the doctrine of virtue, 73
  going beyond, 21
  in Heidegger's thought, 141
  overcoming of, 16
  positive link between Heidegger and, 16
  positive links to, 4
  Schweitzer's, 97
  separation from ethics, 15
  thinkers with a robust, 100
  as what is unknowable, 74
mind, grasping ideas, 10
Mind and Morals, 126
mind-body problem, 10
mind-independent primary qualities, 111
mind-independent values
  ethical realism requiring correspondence with, 143
  none for Rorty, 110
  not existing, 106
mode, in terms of a manner of being, 29
modern world, increases propensity towards mental illness, 46
"moral acquisition device," 119
moral agents, respect between, 25
moral behavior, 4, 116, 120
moral cognition, 122
moral development, 128
Moral Development of the Child, The (Piaget), 78
moral emotions, 118
moral facts, 140
moral feelings, 26, 127
moral fundamentals, 3
moral instinct, evolved, 118

171

Index

moral judgement, emotion and cognition in, 121
moral language
  influencing attitudes, 107
  as prescriptive, 108
moral law, 73, 74
Moral Minds: How Nature Designed our Universal Sense of Right and Wrong (Hauser), 118
moral objectivity, relationship with human desires, 112
moral order, as evidence for God, 76
moral principle, not based on feeling, 73
moral realism
  defined, 132
  described, 2–3
  embracing as plausible, 115
  prospects for, 141–47
  without an expanded ontology, 111
moral realist position, 112
moral realists, defenders of, 3
moral reasoning
  brain research and, 118
  done interpersonally, 120
  resting upon emotions, 127
moral relativism, arguing against, 5
moral relativists, 110, 131
moral responsibility, deriving from human finitude, 27
moral self-knowledge, as beginning of all human wisdom, 74
moral sense, lacking, 127
Moral Sense, The (Wilson), 118
moral systems, 119, 128
moralities, versus ethics, 3
morality
  development of, 79, 126
  growing out of development, 128
  for Kant dealing with the will, 74
  not dealing with happiness, 75
  parameters of in Rawlsian terms, 119
  social and pragmatic origin of, 119
  in terms of laws, 77

morals, as an impossible and unreal category, 108
mothers, importance of ultra-caring, 126
motivating reason, 112
motivation, to be ethical, 30
motivational and basic emotional states, 122
moving something, having power over, 126
mutual trustworthiness, basis for common life, 111
mysterious infinite Will, spiritual self-devotion to, 97
mystic, Schweitzer as a, 98
mystical element, in Heidegger's thought, 10, 21, 69
mystical experience, obtaining self-actualization, 46
mysticism, 90
  ethical content of, 96
  foe of ethics, 96
  living devotion to Being, 96
  not quackery, 38
  overcoming the being-relationship, 5
  requiring little ethical consequences, 96
  Schweitzer's, 93
mythos, of ancient Greece, 17

National Socialist Party, 31
Natural Ethical Facts: Evolution, Connectionism, and Moral Cognition (Casebeer), 116
natural method, employed by Casebeer, 116
natural order, 137
natural selection, fundamental theorem of, 136n115
naturalism
  entailing moral realism, 117
  left adherents of two minds about the arts, 86
  in mathematics, 136

INDEX

Quine's, prompting one to re-look at sociobiology, 135
naturalist, committed to ethical realism, 138
naturalist program, finding a solution to the *is-ought* problem, 134
naturalistic arguments, in favor of moral realism, 144
naturalistic fallacy, 78, 116
naturalized epistemologist, 134
naturalized epistemology
    aiding the sociobiologist, 132
    reasons to adopt, 137
    rendering threat from *is-ought* innocuous, 139
"Naturalized Epistemology" (Quine), 132
nature
    experience of, 28
    forcing to conform to our aims, 100
    orienting ourselves towards, 103
Nature of Mathematical Knowledge, The (Kitcher), 135
Nature of the Child, The (Kagan), 123
nature philosophy, Stoicism as, 95
Nazi party, membership in, 31
Nazi war, Heidegger's support for, 36
Nazism
    charge of, 31–36
    Heidegger's, 2
    Heidegger's attraction to, 34–35
    indicating errors in philosophy, 34
    meaning to Heidegger, 33
    national and social component of, 33
negative argument, of the naturalist program, 134
negative sublime, experience of, 80
neocortex, 120
nervous system, 120, 131
neural processing, about relations to other people, 127
neuroethical reasons, buoying up Heidegger's reading of Kant, 144
neuro-ethicists, giving credence to Heidegger's strategy, 127
neuroethics, 115–30
neurosis, as breakdown in behavior, 43
Nietzsche, "The wasteland grows," 19
Nietzsche Lectures, 36
non-German folk, exclusion of, 33
non-moral reason, 77
normative prohibitions, conformity with, 122
"nothing is without a why," 62
novel events, fear of, 124
"now," contingent upon the advent of the clock, 50

objective (*sophia*) knowledge, 50
objectivity, with reason, 83
objects, dichotomy with representational thinking, 15
obscurity, charge of, 36–39
On Heidegger's Nazism and Philosophy (Rockmore), 33
one-being, separating from many-beings, 69
"Only a God Can Save Us Now," 35
ontic truths, principle of reason seeming to disclose, 61
ontical truth, described, 59
ontological, as fundamental, 60
ontological difference, 11
    as a consequent to the very structure of Dasein, 59
    dissolving radical, 70
    as a distinction of being from beings, 66, 67
    Heidegger's employment of, 59
    Heidegger's genealogy of, 60
    hiding spectre of impossibility of ontology, 59
    implying a similitude of beings and being, 69
    mitigating radical, 69
    as an outcome of the structure of Dasein, 68

Index

ontological difference *(continued)*
    posing a problem for ontology, 57–59
    as a "problem," 66
    remaining, 67
    solving the problem of, 143
    suggesting conceptually distinct categories, 63–64
ontological divided, united by reason, 65
ontological similarity, 57, 142
onto-theology, 69
opportunism, 34
oppressed, concern for, 99
optimism, requiring a metaphysical commitment, 138
optimistic case, *is* and *ought* as co-extensive, 138
ordinary ethics, avoiding, 56
ordinary time, 51, 53–54
origin, coming to meet us from the future, 20
"Origin of the Work of Art, The" 66
original time, 28
originary *ethos*, 22
Out of My Life and Thought: An Autobiography (Schweitzer), 93
outside time, 10
overcoming (*Überwildung*), of inclination by reason, 74
Oxford Lectures on Poetry (Bradley), 89

pain
    not social, 127
    not wishing to avoid it, 117
panentheism, 98
pantheism
    distinguished from panentheism, 70
    of Indian thought, 99
    Schweitzer critical of, 97–98
pantheist, Heidegger as, 70
pantheistic experience of nature, setting things right, 100
Parmenides, 11, 14, 17

particulars (practice), making judgements about, 85
particulars and universals, as illuminating each other, 91–92
passions, far from arbitrary, 144
Passions of the Soul (Descartes), 82
path, submissive nature of being on, 18
peak experiences, 45, 142
personal and impersonal dilemmas, interplay between, 121
personal disposition, 35
personal moral dilemmas, 120, 121
personal welfare, amygdale's role in, 123
pessimistic case, of *is-ought* conflict, 138
PFC (prefrontal cortex), 122, 130
phenomenology, pushing to its limit, 14
philosopher of ethics, 45
philosophers, coming to terms with modern science, 30
philosophical problems, resulting from linguistic confusion, 107
philosophy, importance of, 12–13
The Philosophy of Civilization (Schweitzer), 94, 99
physical death. *See* death
physical laws, acquiring from regularity of experiences, 78
Physics (Aristotle), 43
physis, 14, 28
Piaget, 78–79, 125
Plato
    to know the good is to do it, 117
    the object holy trinity of, 90
    in *The Republic*, 129
    two worlds, 50
Platonism, Heidegger seeking to avoid, 100
Platonist metaphysics, Heidegger avoiding, 28
play, suggesting the giving of being to beings, 63

"Poem to an Unknown Soldier," 41
poetry, as a way to truth for Hegel, 88
political romanticism, Heidegger's, 31
politics
    Heidegger's, 142
    separating Heidegger's philosophy from, 36
positive argument, of the naturalist program, 134
post-modern strategy, example of, 109
practical and theoretical reason, attempting to distinguish between, 80
practice, paying attention to, 113
practices-cum-knowledge, 139
preferred behaviors, leaving genetic imprint, 133
prefrontal cortex (PFC), 122, 130
"preontological," understanding of, 59
present (present-ation), 51
present-at-hand (*Vorhanden*), viewing into what is read-at-hand (*Zuhanden*), 14
presentness (*Anwesneheit*), related to being, 10–11
Pre-Socratics
    appropriating, 14
    history of philosophy after, 15
    as primordial thinkers, 11–12
primitive, rule-based (collective) societies, 79
primitive areas, of the brain maturing first, 126
primitive emotions, 119–20, 144
primordial ethics, rooted in a world of practices, 56
primordial temporality, time as, 11
primordial time
    arriving at ordinary time as a succession of nows, 53
    Heidegger proposed to go back to, 51
    presupposed for any conception of time, 54
    recovery of, 49
    retrospective to the loss of, 50
    seeming to collapse into idealism, 54
Principia Ethica (Moore), 116
principium grande, 61
principle of reason. *See also* reason
    hearing in two ways, 64
    kinship to being, 62
    not shedding light on how to understand ontological difference, 61
    as a principle of being, 64
principle of sufficient reason, 61, 68
problems, engaging in inquiry solving, 131
production, through freedom, 85
professional, being, 104–5
protention, 51
psychological development, seminal phases, 79
psychopaths
    case of, 78
    characteristics of, 127
    having moral reasoning without emotions, 120
public performance, 125
public policy, tension with personal experiences, 104
public-private split, taking to its logical end, 105

quackery, theme of dogging Heidegger, 38
Question Concerning Technology, The, 18
question of being, forgetting of, 19
"Question of Ethics in Heidegger's Thought, The" (Boelen), 23
questions, as obscure, 38
Quine's naturalism, 139

radical idealism, as the most robust realism, 92
rational (ethical) acts, resting on the passions, 129

Index

rational agents, requiring them to be abstract citizens, 77
"rational cognition," fundamental principle of, 61
rational thinking, putting faith in, 95
readings, by Heidegger, 38
realism-idealism debates, evading, 16
realist ethics, supporting the idea of, 5
reality, Thoreau craving, 102
reason. *See also* principle of reason
    actions of as good, 84
    allowing to be both universal and particular, 65
    allowing to distinguish what is good or bad, 84
    as being, 69
    being and, 62
    for beings as being, 65
    connecting to being, 65
    construed instrumentally, 61
    Heidegger's exploration and excavation of, 60
    of a particular thing, 65
    perfecting, 84
    as a source of knowledge, 86
    Spinoza prioritizing over the emotions, 84
    in terms of why, 62
reason/ground/essence, exploration of, 66
reasoning, overemphasized at the expense of intuition, 120
reciprocity, 79
regionalism, of being, 11
"the relation of men to men," ethics dealing with, 74
relationship to being, seeking through beings, 100
religion, displacement of, 30
Renewal of the Heidegger-Kant Dialogue: Action, Thought, and Responsibility, The (Schalow), 27
Republic, The (Plato), 129
resoluteness, specific present belonging to, 29
respect (*Achtung*)
    versus duty (*Dienst*), 81
    Kant's entire ethics resting on, 25
    meaning responsibility towards oneself, 26
retention, 51
reverence for life
    concept of, 97–101
    ethic of, 96
    as an example of "letting beings be," 93
    helping elucidate a Heideggerian ethic, 99
    principle of, 95
rhesus monkeys, experiments with, 126
"right," related to a "good," 112
Rilke, Rainer Maria, 40, 41, 42
Rockmore, Tom, 33
romantic motivations, 5, 142
Romantic Movement, Heidegger in, 142
romantic nationalism, motivated Nazism, 33
romanticism
    confronting the dark side of, 31
    as desire to commune with ancestry and native land, 32
    Heidegger's, 12
    moving in two directions, 34
    unrepentant in Heidegger, 40
romantics
    complaints of with modernity, 105
    dream and the tragedy of, 41
    taking up the idea of a fall from grace, 81
Rome, fall of, 42–43
Rorty, contemporary American pragmatist, 109–10
rose
    blooming because of itself, 69
    paying no attention to its grounds, 62

Index

rules, internalizing as our own, 79
Russell, Bertrand, 36

Schelling, treatise on human freedom, 20
Schweitzer
    connections with Heidegger, 99
    ethics of, 93–105
    material progress making civilization more difficult, 93–97
    representing a romantic grain of thought, 101
    skeptical about what mysticism can offer the ethicist, 96
"Schweitzer, Jainism, and Reverence for Life" (Baram), 98
science
    acquiring reverence for wonders of nature, 136
    as basic event of our spiritual-national existence, 32
    falling upon its own keen sword, 42
    modern, 30
    relation to ethics, 116
    statements for and against, 35
    using to justify ethics, 131
scientific disputes, as disagreements about beliefs, 107
scientism, 43, 113
secondary qualities, 111
secure attachment, not beneficial indefinitely, 124
security, increasing, 43
self, first phase in establishing, 124
self-actualization, 45, 46, 142
"The Self-Determination of the German University" (speech), 32, 35
self-esteem, increasing, 43
sensory-motor schema, 124
separation from being, as a "default," 20
serotonin, lower levels of, 126
Shaftsbury, Lord, Schweitzer's praise for, 95
shame, 123

Sheppard of being, man as, 70
Silesius, Angelus, 62, 65
Singer, Peter, 78
social basis, of perception and knowledge, 118
social context. *See also* context
    driving research and ethics, 131
    in which morality develops, 126
social factors, shaping perception, 128
social norms, varying across cultures, 123
social program, in Christianity, 98–99
social semantic knowledge, 122
societies
    expressing ethical principles in law, 97
    organized around kinship and children, 119
sociobiologist, 132
sociobiology
    consistent with ethical realism, 135
    defending, 131
    explaining different regimes of ethical governance, 138
    not accounting for altruism, 137
    revised, 136–37
socio-emotional responses, 121
solidarity, aesthetic appreciation bound by, 87
Sophocles, 21
soul, 9, 11
Spengler
    committed to the notion of destiny, 43
    on "decline of the West," 19
    drawing parallels to, 142
    "metaphysical structure" of history, 42
Spinoza, account of beauty, 83–84
spiritual, appearing in sensuous shape in art, 88
spiritual decadence, born into a period of, 95
Stadelmann, Rudolf, 40

Index

standardization, provided by a shared measure of time, 52
starlings, flying close together, 133
state of fallenness, Dasein's, 53
Stoicism, fundamental thought og, 95
story of being, Heidegger's, 41
Stroop task, 121
student, allowing "to let learn," 19
subjective (*doxa*) knowledge, 50
subjectivism, 15, 87, 110
subjectivity
    Heidegger's critique of, 22
    lies with the senses, 83
    revaluation of the role of, 91
subjectivity or objectivity, problem of time's, 54–55
sublime
    dealing with "quantity," 85
    elicited by greatest works of art, 85
    experience of, 80–81, 100
    as foundation of a Heideggerian ethics, 92
    nature of, 80
    as a "negative feeling" for Kant, 85
    requiring a submission of will to recognition, 80
"sublime indeterminacy," 90
submission, key notion of, 23
"submission" theme, in relation to being, 20
submissive consequences, of mystical experience, 100
submissiveness, punctuating Heidegger's comments, 18–19
success policy, acting to avoid pain, 109
sufficient reason, principle of, 60
synaptic connections, pruning of, 115

tactile creatures, children as, 104
Taoism, 23
task mastery, motive for, 123
teaching placement, in junior-senior kindergarten, 104
technology, Heidegger's critique of, 35, 46
telos, 26, 68
temperament, shaped in early childhood, 125
temporality
    as the basis of the question of being, 29
    unity of already present, 52
"thankful" thinking, 19
themes, in Heidegger's writings, 16
theoretical reason, postulates of, 76
theory of mind, 82, 118
things, thinking about in terms of time, 51–52
thinking, Heidegger on, 18–21
thinking of being, as separate from particular beings, 11
Thoreau, 100–102
thought and being, union of, 29
"Thoughts" (Frege), 90
time
    accompanying motion, 50
    as an analogy for being-question relating to ethics, 49
    as a "convention," 54
    dealing with in terms of the future, 53
    different conceptions of, 54
    as either right or wrong, 52
    first encountered when we deal with things, 51
    having no length according to Heidegger, 50
    Heidegger's discourse on, 9
    as an image of eternity, 50
    including as the basis of ethics, 28
    as a means to an end, 54
    measuring, 52, 53
    never knowing what it is in-itself precisely, 56
    not objective or subjective, 55
    notion of, 10
    present-at-hand, 55

Index

as the *a priori* of the ego, 26
problem of the nature of, 28
as a public phenomenon, 52
ready-at-hand in-order-to, 54
role in human development, 29
using according to a certain dating system, 56
what is in, 27–28
what is outside of, 27
time-slices, 50
"To the Virgin Mary" (poem), 39
"total person," looking to, 46
"total personality," Maslow concentrated on, 43
tragedy, Hegel's account of, 88
transcendence, possibility of, 11
transcendental (ontological) grounds, 60
transcendental approach, 60
transcendental argument, 54
transcendental grounds, primordiality of, 58
"transformation," required to be able to equate both being and reason, 63
Treaty of Versailles, redress from, 33
truth
  dual notion of, 60
  manifest in history, 13
  as the property of a proposition, 15
  representational theory of, 21
  "revealed in real appearance to our external perception," 88
  separation from beauty, 87
  as the way being is disclosed to us, 15–16
truth character, of being, 11

"uncanny" moment, art providing for Kant, 90
uncarved block, as one ideal in Taoism, 23
unity
  of the idea of being, 11
  between nature and us, 14
  of the soul, 42
universal Dasein, using time, 53
universal ethics, attempts to justify, 118
"universal moral grammar," 119
universal moral rules, not presupposing, 122
universal will-to-life, mystical union with, 98
universality
  of aesthetic judgement, 86
  splintered through the prism of history for Hegel, 89
universals (theory), of Kant, 85
unnatural fallacy, 1, 78
untruth (*falsum*), Roman conception of, 12
utilitarians, trying to formalize the practice of ethics, 30

values
  at the base of ethics, 145
  not mind-independent, 113
  as psychological or sociological judgments, 107
  serving functions that are part of collective practices, 145
  as subject dependent and objective, 113
Vaulting Ambition: Sociobiology and the Quest for Human Nature (Kitcher), 136
veridical character of being, 11
virtue ethics, 2
virtue policy, proving to be the only success policy, 109
virtue theory, pragmatic neo-Aristotelian, 116
vision, articulating a moment of, 29
Voronezh Notebooks, 41

war, as the will-to-power and the oblivion of being, 36
Watson, Paul, 102
West, unique in having a history, 42

Index

Western metaphysics, Heidegger's critique of, 143
Western ontology, Heidegger's deconstruction of the history of, 16
Western thought, recovering the inception of, 9
what is given, as important, 20
why, rose without, 62
why or reason, of beings, 64
Williams, Bernard, 77
will-to-live, manifesting itself, 95
"will-to-love," experience of God as, 96
withdrawal of being, 13, 14, 100
Wolffian framework, of one (being) and many (beings), 58
world
    as an idea in the mind of God, 66
    is an expression of being, 13
    something common to all things in, 58
World War I, redress from, 33
"worldhood," time's relation to, 55
worldviews, notion of differing, 89

www.ingramcontent.com/pod-product-compliance
Lightning Source LLC
Chambersburg PA
CBHW051744230426
43670CB00012B/2151